I0568147

OUT OF THE WOODS

AN INSPIRATIONAL SELF-HELP MEMOIR

DR. HAWK M. HORVATH

Copyright © 2022 by Dr. Hawk M. Horvath

All rights reserved.

No part of this book may be reproduced in any form or by any electronic or mechanical means, including information storage and retrieval systems, without written permission from the author, except for the use of brief quotations in a book review.

Please note that the names of the church members and the location of the churches have been changed out of respect for those well-meaning people. Also, note that at that time the author's name was Rev. Nancy Jo Horvath. It was legally changed to Rev. Dr. Hawk M. Horvath in 2018. These are one and the same person.

This book is dedicated to Barbara Zurn and Zach Zurn, who saw me through this challenging time of life. In addition, it is dedicated to my spirit guides, spirit animals, teachers/mentors, angels, and the blessed ancestors who continue to guide my way.

CONTENTS

FOREWORD

Choke...chug...sputter. I knew I should have put gas in the Jeep. Choke... chug...sputter. The yellow warning light had come on days earlier. Still, I chose to park it in front of the house for not one but three days. Choke... chug...sputter....VROOM! Something connected but I'm operating on fumes and need to get to a gas station quickly.

Now, what's my best course of action? Keeping the air conditioning off might buy me some distance. Ugh. Driving in triple-digit temperatures is not a pleasant thought. Sweltering air flows into the hot vehicle through the open window. Driving slowly makes more sense than driving faster because the faster I drive the more gas I use. Creeping along puts my nerves on edge. I'm hot, I'm stressed, and I like I said, I'm running on fumes.

It would be so easy to turn on the air conditioning, hit the gas and get to the gas station quickly. But running on fumes requires extra precautions. Here's hoping those precautions aren't too little too late.

Had the proper maintenance been done in the first place I wouldn't be in this boat...er...uh...Jeep. Proper maintenance shouldn't be so difficult, should it?

It seems to me that you just need to do a few things and be intentional about them. According to the manual, when providing proper maintenance,

I need to be aware of fluid levels, the brake system, windshield wipers and the electrical system.

The manual doesn't mention fuel. Oh, wait a minute. Here it is on page 116 under "Starting and Operating." Listed last among other ways to minimize the possibility of catalytic converter damage, the words, "Do not allow the vehicle to run out of fuel" finally speak to me. OK. What's a catalytic converter and why do I care about its damage? All I know is that it's 108 degrees and I don't want to sit alone on the side of the road with an empty gas tank.

As I get to the stop sign the engine sputters again. I pray there will be enough fumes to get me around the corner and into the gas station. I'm not out of the woods yet. Careful not to hit the gas pedal too hard, I turn the corner. One more sputter and I'm coasting up to the pump.

I made it! I'm out of the woods.

At least for now.

PREFACE

Choke....chug...sputter. This was the sound of my spiritual life one bright summer morning. I knew I should have done something when I realized I was beginning to feel drained. Instead, I put my self-care aside and kept plugging along. Then when life heated up, as it has a way of doing, I realized I needed to start up my spiritual engine.

Proper maintenance? Well, of course! It sounds so easy to be intentional about the basics: eat right, get plenty of sleep, take vitamins, exercise, and reserve time for daily prayer and devotional. But here's the truth of the matter: it isn't as easy as it sounds, or at least it isn't for me.

It's incredible to me how easy it is to run out of fuel, not just in the Jeep but also in my spiritual life. I would find it sadly interesting to know how many days out of a year I spiritually run on fumes. Empty, tired, frustrated. How does this happen? Why aren't I better at regular maintenance?

Out of the Woods is about a time when I found myself in a crisis of spirit. You hear about someone having a mental breakdown. An emotional breakdown. A nervous breakdown. Well, I experienced a *spiritual* breakdown. I was at the end of my rope, questioning my entire relationship with God.

"So, what's the big deal?" you ask.

I am a pastor. That sounds bad, doesn't it? How could a minister allow such a thing to happen? After all, aren't clergy supposed to be a spiritual cut above the rest? Don't we have a special connection with God?

NO. Ministers are only human. We laugh, we cry, we bleed, we die. We have the same spiritual connection that everyone else has to God. With the proper maintenance, we too can have thriving spiritual lives. Without that maintenance, we can find ourselves running on fumes.

When training to become clergy, I was taught to be ready to preach, pray or die at a moment's notice. I was not taught, however, how to have a personal spiritual life. This lapse in my training and education came back to haunt me.

INTO THE WOODS

THE CALL

In the early nineties, I accepted a call to a pulpit near the panhandle of Oklahoma. Prior to moving to Evanston, my family and I located a beautiful house and put a bid on it. We then put our beautiful old Victorian home on the market and, as we expected, it sold quickly.

Moving is never easy, and as a seasoned pastor, this wasn't the first time my family and I had moved. We'd enjoyed Grove City with its thriving congregation, but my three-year contact had ended, and it was time for the next pastor to come in who would take the congregation to the next level of ministry and growth.

The thought of leaving our lovely suburban home for a city a thousand miles away brought great sadness. On the other hand, this smaller congregation was looking for a pastor who could help them with the same work I had completed in Grove City. I knew we would adjust to the changes over time. We always had before.

This time, however, we had a new addition to the family. Our dogs and cats had moved with us in the past, but our son Zachary had just turned four and he had never lived in any house but the blue house.

"I don't want to go in the big truck, Mama! I want to stay in ours blue house," he wailed one evening at the dinner table.

"But don't you want to see your new bedroom, Zach? We're taking your car bed and all your toys with us too," I explained for what seemed like the thousandth time as I filled his glass with milk.

"I like the blue house," he whimpered.

"So do I," whispered my life-partner Barb as she passed me the bread.

"Not you too," I protested. "C'mon. Cut me a break here."

"I know it's a God-thing," she replied. "I know you have to answer your

call and I respect that. I've been with you too many years to think any different. But I love this old house. I love the people in our church and the friends I've made at work."

"Sorry," I said. "I know it's hard on you too. But things will work out great in Evanston. The people seem terrific at Trinity Church, and we'll soon feel like a part of the church family. You'll see."

"Oh, before I forget," she said, "Brad called. He wants you to call him back."

"He wants to know why we're moving to Oklahoma instead of back to Minnesota?"

"You guessed it!" she replied. "No big surprise there. He and Gary are always hoping we'll head back home one of these days."

"You explained to them that my call is to Trinity, right?"

"Well, what do you think?" she retorted with a grin. "For about the umpteenth time!"

"Ok, I'll give him a call this evening."

"Do you ever think we'll move back home?" she asked, her voice thick with hesitation.

"Before retirement you mean? I can't imagine it. But miracles do happen. Let's leave it in God's hands, OK?" I replied as I rose to clear the dishes from the table.

"You do the dishes and I'll pack another box," she said.

"Does that include cleaning up our son as well?" I retorted. He had just dropped a blob of chocolate ice cream on his lap.

She smiled as she came around the table and half-hugged me,

reaching across me with one arm to grab yet another empty box waiting to be filled.

Barb and I had been together for just over ten years. I suspected that she knew me better than I knew myself. I remember her strong resolve the day I came home and told her that I had sensed a distinct call from God that my ministry in Grove City was coming to an end. Her face had slowly filled with sadness, and though a tear rolled down her cheek, she said, "I trust that God will lead us to the right church."

How I wished I held the same strong faith she did.

PAJAMA PARTY FROM HELL

"Nancy," Barb said with a deep intake of breath, "you'd better sit down. I just had a call from the realtor in Evanston. Our financing isn't going through."

"What?" I shouted. I was packing the truck we would be driving to Oklahoma.

"The inspectors found structural problems, and our financing just fell apart."

"Oh no!" I cried. "What are we going to do? The movers are going to be here first thing in the morning. If we cancel now, we lose twenty-five percent of our money."

"We can't cancel now," she replied. "The buyers plan to move into this house in three days."

"What are we going to do?" I asked again.

"I think we'd better start praying," she replied.

I couldn't think of another thing to do as tears of frustration sprang to my eyes.

I would love to say that this was the only stressful part of our move, but I can't. This move was all about stress. Like the call I got from my mother one sunny afternoon, two weeks earlier, as I was filling another box with books.

"Well," she said with relief in her voice, "We got Mick into a nursing home yesterday. My pastor spent the entire day with me, helping me fill out the paperwork. I don't know what I'd have done without him."

"Oh, that's great, Mom," I said distractedly. "I'm sure you're relieved to have him in a good home."

"I sure wish I could handle him myself," she said sadly, "but I just can't. He needs more care than I can give him."

That was the truth. My brother Mick had been a violent alcoholic for as long as I could remember. Through the years he'd lost his family, countless jobs, his friends, and his self-respect. Sitting on a park bench panhandling money was the big event of his day until he became so sick he ended up in a hospital emergency room. He had cancer in his lungs and it was spreading at a rapid pace. Chemotherapy had prolonged his life for six months past that diagnosis, but it was too little too late. He was on a rapid decline.

Although it was good news to learn he was in a nursing home, it still burdened my heart to know that he likely had less than a year to live. I knew that Mom was stressed, and I saw no reason to add to that stress by telling her about the lack of a house waiting for us in Oklahoma. I chose to wait for a better time that never seemed to come. I'd talk to her during the drive. And maybe there'd be better news about a house. Maybe.

Zach continued to be adamant that he wasn't leaving the blue house.

"No! I don't want to go to a new house! I want to stay here in my room in ours blue house."

"Well," I said choosing my words carefully, "Mommy and I think we should go to a different house than the one with the big windows. Why don't we pick out a new house when we all get to Evanston?"

"No!" he wailed. "I want to stay in the blue house!"

Barb and I tried to cajole him, humor him, excite him, but to no avail. After we found the poor little guy sitting in the backyard with the dogs, crying as all the possessions he held dear were loaded into that monstrous truck, we called a friend from church who came to take him to her house while the rest of the truck was packed.

On top of it all, our cat Toby had cystitis. When this large yellow-and-white beauty became stressed, he relieved himself everywhere but in the litter box. In addition, we had two tiger-striped cats and two Labrador Retrievers that were beginning to show signs of stress with all the changes in the house.

The last night in the blue house was memorable. Without a stick of furniture left in our home, every possession we owned packed away in the moving truck, we sat there on the floor eating take-out pizza.

"Zach, we're having a pajama party in the living room tonight!" Barb said. "We'll all sleep on the floor in sleeping bags in front of the fireplace," I added. "Doesn't that sound like fun?"

"Yes," he replied with reluctance. "But I don't want to leave the blue house."

I knew exactly how he felt.

"It'll all be OK, Nanc," Barb whispered a few hours later as we hunkered down on the hard wood floor in our sleeping bags.

"Do you really believe that or are you just trying to convince yourself?" I asked with a forced smile.

"It always works out," she said, her voice low. "God has never failed us yet."

"I agree," I said. "But I sure wish God would let me in on the grand scheme. I can't believe we're pulling out of here tomorrow and moving to a city where we don't even have a house to live in."

"Well, the people from the new church said they'd work on some options for us. Let's give them a chance. We're supposed to get a hotel room on the edge of Evanston, then give the president of the trustees a call. They'll have a plan. Let's just trust."

"Sometimes I think *you* should be the pastor," I said with conviction. "You certainly are the faith-keeper in this family."

"No way!" she exclaimed. "I could never do what you do. Now let's get some sleep, hon. Tomorrow's a big day."

I was lost in my thoughts before falling asleep, but I thought I heard her crying quietly to herself.

BIG BAD MAMA

I awoke several hours later with my back aching from the hard floor. The fire had long since gone out, and Barb and little Zachary were sleeping peacefully. As I rolled over, I smelled something foul. Sitting straight up I realized that the top of my sleeping bag was wet. Poor Toby had reached his max in stress and had boldly urinated where no self-respecting cat would urinate-- all over my sleeping bag.

It was the last straw. Tears streamed down my face as I realized that we couldn't possibly take him with us. If he was this stressed out at the beginning of the trip, how would he deal with two nights in a hotel along the way, and yet another hotel when got to town?

Barb woke up to find me holding our precious kitty trying to hold back the sobs.

"We don't even know where we'll end up," I choked. The last call from Trinity had mentioned that some folks might let us move in with them until we found a house. "We can't have him doing his business in hotel rooms and other people's homes. Oh Barb, this is just too much."

"Let me call Katie from work," she suggested. "She's said several times, over the years, that she'd love to have a cat like him."

We got on the road before noon, the sun blazing overhead, but we were a sad group of travelers. I kept thinking about Abraham and Sarah from Genesis chapter twelve when God said to Abraham, "Prepare to go to a place I will show you." I had thought we knew the place we were going, but now without a home, we were more like pilgrims setting out for a foreign land. Where in the world was God taking us?

It took two days to get to the hotel just outside of Evanston. You've never truly moved until you've done so with two dogs, two cats and an angry pre-schooler. Adding insult to injury Zach told everyone we met, from waitresses to people at rest stops, about his plight.

"We're moving," he said to one unsuspecting waitress.

"I can see that," she replied politely as she prepared to take our order. "My, but that's a big truck. Are you excited?"

"No. I want to go back home to the blue house. Mama said we have to move. God said so."

"Oh, well I'll bet your new house will be very nice too," she said with a curious look our way.

"We don't have a new house," he said sadly.

"I see," she replied, unsure of where to go with this. "Well, I can see you have puppies going with you. Wasn't that you out there walking those pretty dogs? Isn't that nice to have your whole family going along?"

"But Mama left Toby at home because he peed on her sleeping bag. Now he can't go."

"Goodness, you're having a tough day, aren't you, little fella? How about I give you a large glass of chocolate milk instead of a small one? On the house," she said as she threw an accusatory glance our way.

"And all my toys are in that truck. I want to go home to the blue house!" He broke into tears yet again.

This scenario played itself out with anyone who would acknowledge him when he stated, "We're moving." Barb and I began to dread the sight of any new unsuspecting person he might bait. I hated for people to believe that I was the dreadful *mama*. I remember a lady at a rest stop who sat right down on a bench with him to listen to his sad plight. She looked at both Barb and me with a questioning glare.

Then much to my shock, he said with despair, "I hope I never pee on Mama's sleeping bag."

Barb quickly said, "C'mon, Zach. *Mama* and I are going to the truck."

"Thanks a lot," I said. "That woman's out for blood!"

"Yeah," she grinned. "Well, I sure didn't want to be the mama in that moment."

"Do you really think he's afraid I'd leave him behind if he had an accident on my sleeping bag?"

"Hard to tell what that baby thinks right now," she replied. "But I suggest you reassure him at your earliest opportunity."

TACTICAL ERRORS

S ettling into a house that is not your own is unsettling. While grateful for a place to stay during our house hunting, we worried about the cats, worried about the dogs, worried little Zach would break something. Barb started her new job as planned, and I was left each day with our gracious hosts, their three dogs and two cats, our own frightened and confused pets, and a very angry little boy.

The highlight of my first two days was frenzied phone conversations with our realtor. He had several homes for us to look at, and we were chomping at the bit to get into our own space.

Then, just three days after we arrived, I received a call from my mother in Pennsylvania.

"Honey, this is Mom. I'm afraid I have some bad news."

"Oh no, Mom, is it about Mick?" I could hear her crying softly on the other end of the line.

Mick and I had never been close. There was a whopping twelve-year age difference between us, and he moved out of the house when he was sixteen years old. Always the renegade, Mick had been the cause of more than his share of my mother's gray hair. Even so, my mother loved him with a fierceness that only a mother can know. My heart went out to her as only a daughter's can.

"Do you think you can make it home for his funeral, Nancy?" she asked.

I closed my eyes and struggled back tears of my own. "I sure want to, but you know our situation here, Mom. We still don't have a house, and Barb just started work."

"Well, honey," she replied with a newfound strength, "I'll send airfare for you to come. Bring Zach too. I understand that Barb can't get away right now, but please try to come. Nancy, I really need you here."

After we hung up, I called the president of the trustees to say I would not be coming to the Bible study that evening. I shared with him that my brother had just passed away and I was in a bit of a quandary as to what to do. He offered me his support and condolences and then said he would call the other trustees and people in leadership to let them know.

Within fifteen minutes the telephone rang. It was one of the church leaders calling to confirm the news.

"Well, I'm sorry about your brother and all, but you can't mean to tell me that you're going to go to Pennsylvania now?" she stated bluntly. "You just got here. The church needs you."

"Of course," I replied. "But my mother also needs me."

"But we paid to move you here. We're offering you a nice home to stay in with some good people. You can't turn your back on us now that you've finally gotten here," she retorted.

"I'll fly," I said with determination. "That way I'll only be there for three to four days."

"I just can't believe you're planning to leave after you just got here," she griped. "This is a real problem."

While I was taken back by her manner, I also understood her position. The church had waited for months for us to arrive. They were planning a huge welcoming celebration on Sunday. What would it look like if I wasn't there?

I found myself thinking about my family in Pennsylvania. My

mother needed me, but truth be told, there were others who could be there for her. Or at least that's how I rationalized it. Besides, I knew that I didn't want to leave Barb, with all of our pets, living in someone else's home. I also knew that she needed to work and I needed to spend time with the realtor finding us a house.

"What am I going to do?" I whispered as we lay there in someone else's bed in someone else's house.

Barb reached over to take my hand. "You just do what you have to do, Nanc."

"I should be there." The pain tore through me at the thought of telling my mother I couldn't be with her. "My mother needs me."

"But remember, there are others who can be there for her," she sighed. "You have two other brothers."

"But she asked me to come," I moaned.

"Listen," she replied convincingly, "you know that I trust your judgment. I can hold down the fort here. Go if you need to go."

She was so understanding that I felt all the more guilty. In fact, I wasn't sure that I trusted my own judgment.

After weighing the pros and cons, I decided not to go to Pennsylvania. I had a moment of dread, wishing I could somehow be in two places at one time. As I picked up the phone to return a call from the realtor faces flashed through my mind: my mother's face, Mick's face, and Toby the cat's face.

And so, I began my new ministry by making some very large tactical errors. These errors would not be without repercussions.

CASUALTIES

Three weeks later we moved into a house of our own. Thank God for the sellers who allowed us to begin transferring our things out of storage and into the house before we signed the paperwork. I will never forget our first night there. We slept on the hide-a-bed in the living room. It was so packed with boxes that we couldn't even see the fireplace, but it was home. Our home!

As we settled in, I began to wonder what I'd been thinking when I left Toby behind. It felt as if we were missing a family member in the midst of all of this transition. I'd search for Tiger and Mikki, the other cats inside the house, then realized that I was also searching for the one who was no longer with us. I missed him.

We called Katie, who had kept him for us, and learned that after a week or so of adjusting to the new house, he'd settled in beautifully. I was happy for him but sad for us. I deeply regretted my decision to leave him behind.

It was about this time that I began having recurring dreams of my mother and recently deceased brother. They were together, in a deep forest, searching with flashlights for someone.

I kept running after them, calling out, "Who are you looking for?"

As they'd turn around to see who was coming after them my mother would yell, "Nancy!" I would immediately wake up in a cold sweat. I had no idea what the dreams meant, only that they were very disturbing.

I jokingly called our home the Little House on the Prairie. It was on a large lot in desperate need of landscaping. The house was smaller than what we originally wanted, but as my mother said over the phone, "any port in a storm." Unfortunately, the storm would quickly become an Oklahoma cyclone.

It was one thing for my brother to die, but it was almost as if this tragedy set off a domino effect. Within two months of our arrival, Allie, one of our yellow labs, became acutely ill and died in my arms on the way to the emergency pet clinic.

The day had been unusually hot, even by Oklahoma standards. My mother had flown into the local airport that morning, about an hour's drive away. It was wonderful to see her, and we fell into one another's arms with tears of joy. This was our first reunion following Mick's death, and we spent the afternoon reflecting upon better days when my dad was alive and the family intact.

Zachary remembered Grandma Peg, much to her delight. He sat glued to her as they watched The Jungle Book that evening. He fell asleep on her lap only after we promised that Grandma would still be with us the next morning.

We never expected that Allie wouldn't. She hadn't been sick, and she was too young to die of natural causes. At 11:30 that night, Barb woke with a start.

"I hear something strange outside," she said nervously as she shook me awake.

I threw on my bathrobe and headed for the back door. That's when the most pitiful sound I'd ever heard reached my ears.

"It's obviously a wounded animal," I whispered. "Where are Sunny and Allie?"

"They're out there," Barb replied.

We turned on the backyard light and proceeded carefully, suspecting that the dogs had a raccoon or armadillo cornered in the fenced yard. Much to our dismay, we saw Sunny standing over the moaning form on the ground.

"Call the emergency vet!" I screamed as I raced to my baby's side. Allie and I had shared seven years of her life since we'd found the litter of four-week-old pups at the bottom of a cliff in the Allegheny Mountains of Pennsylvania. She and Sunny were litter mates, and no dogs were closer than the two of them.

When Barb returned, fully clothed, and said the vet was waiting for us, I took a moment to throw on some jeans and a t-shirt. I woke Mom and hastily explained what was going on.

"Oh, no!" she exclaimed. "What can I do to help?

"Stay here with Zach," I replied as I tied my sneakers. "If he wakes up, tell him Allie got sick and we took her to the doctor."

Running out the door I saw that Barb had placed a towel around Allie's body. The poor pup was totally unresponsive except for the horrible moaning. I picked her up in the towel and carried her to the passenger side of the Jeep. Holding her tightly against my chest and talking to her nonstop, I gave Barb the signal to hit it!

"I can't believe she's gone." I cried as Barb drove us home later that night.

"Me neither," Barb said choking back her tears. "I'm so sorry, Nanc. I know she was your special dog."

"What will we tell Zach in the morning?" I asked. "I mean, one day he's playing with her and the next day we have to tell him she died. He'll probably think she pooped on my sleeping bag." I tried to wipe the tears from my face but couldn't seem to keep up with them.

"He's not going to blame you," she replied. "We'll just have to do our best with it. Death is part of life. It's a natural lesson for him. We'll help him through this. Thank God your mother's visiting this week of all weeks."

"What about Sunny?" I asked quietly

"She's going to be lost." Barb sobbed as the tears cascaded down her face.

We were silent for the rest of the ride home. I hugged the empty towel and Allie's blue collar to my heart as we pulled into the driveway.

"So, can I ask you something before we go inside?" she said.

"Sure," I replied, my voice cracking.

"Why didn't you request an autopsy on Allie?"

I was quiet for a few moments. I didn't know whether to break the news to her or continue to hold it quietly in my heart.

"I've had two hate-filled letters from self-proclaimed Christians in town who apparently are against homosexuals. They obviously have no sense of humor about having a lesbian pastor in their town," I said, my voice dripping with sarcasm.

"Oh my gosh! Why didn't you tell me?" she exclaimed.

"I blew off the first one," I replied. "And I just got the second one yesterday. I didn't say anything because I didn't want to upset Mom. You know how scared she is that someone might hurt me because I'm so openly gay. I planned to talk with you after she went back to Pennsylvania."

"So do you think someone hurt Allie on purpose? Poisoned her or something?" she questioned.

"I don't know," I responded. "I guess with so much going on I don't want to know. Let's just keep a closer eye on Sunny."

As expected, Zachary was horrified. He had struggled with leaving Toby behind and the death of his Uncle Mick. Now our four-year-old faced the death of one of our dogs. We couldn't help noticing that he began watching over Sunny like a hawk. On top of it all, he seemed very uncomfortable with his bedroom. He didn't want to play in it and was scared to go to bed at night. We bought him night lights, dream catchers, and everything else we could think of. No matter. He was just not happy living anywhere but in the "blue house".

THE GRIM REAPER

I wish I could say that leaving the cat behind, my brother's death and the dog's death were the last goodbyes for a while. But no fewer than seventeen deaths touched our family in the next year and a half. Many of them were members of the different churches I had pastored throughout the years. The AIDS crisis was in full swing, and I had already buried way too many men.

"Barb, can you get the phone?" I asked.

"No," she stated. "I can see from the caller ID that it's my sister."

"You love your sister," I laughed.

"Yep, and so do you. You answer the phone," she said jokingly.

"Every time she calls it seems like someone else has died," I sighed.

"I know," Barb said quietly. "I think she's beginning to feel like the grim reaper."

"OK, my turn to answer the phone," I relented. "Hello?"

"Who now?" Barb whispered expectantly.

"Richard's gone. It was pneumocystis pneumonia," I sighed as I handed her the phone. Zach's middle name, Richard, was given to him in honor of this wonderful man who was gone way too soon.

We held each other a little closer that night as we reflected on all those who had left this world over the past months. How could so many leave us at one time?

I only attended the funerals I officiated at Trinity during that year and a half. Despite it being a smaller congregation, we had three funerals.

"Nancy," asked my mother over the phone, "how are you holding up through all this? I know you were really close to some of those people from your former churches."

"Oh, I'm fine Mom. It's just part of being a pastor," I replied, with false bravado.

"But are you getting any help with the grief and loss?" she asked. "That's a lot of death over a short period of time. I don't know how anyone could deal with it, and the workload you pastors carry."

"Not to worry, Mother," I chided her. "It's all a part of the job. I'm good!"

I truly believed I was OK. I believed that I was strong enough to handle all this loss on my own. I was a pastor, after all, and death and dying were part of life. But truthfully, I barely had time to even consider my grief before receiving the news that someone else had died. I was in pain. And I was in denial. I simply couldn't see the long-term effects that loomed in the distance.

The warning light had come on. I was low on fuel, yet I chose to ignore all the signs of trouble.

"I need a project to keep me busy and my mind occupied," I told Barb one bright sunny Oklahoma morning. I had never been much of a gardener, but the Little House on the Prairie was begging for landscaping. I purchased plants and numerous 40-pound bags of soil and mulch and began to counter all those deaths with life. I began creating!

And while I was creating the landscape, I was creating some aches and pains. As a physical therapist, Barb tried to warn me.

"Nancy, you have to slow down. God didn't create the world in a day. We don't need to have the front yard landscaped in a week."

"I know, I know," I replied. "But I'm really getting into this. It's more fun than it is work. Did you see what I put around that tree over by the mailbox?"

"It's looking good," she concurred, glancing at the Oklahoma stone border circling bright yellow pansies. "But please pace yourself. Why don't you use the egg timer and set it for thirty-minute intervals? That way you can fit in some regular breaks. And remember, there's always tomorrow."

It's no surprise that I didn't listen. I was in denial about many of my human limitations. I blew off her suggestions and just kept on hauling dirt and planting flowers and bulbs.

"Hey, at least I'm on my knees," I said kiddingly. "Isn't that where a pastor is supposed to spend her days?"

Barb just shook her head. She knew all she could do was offer suggestions. What I did with those suggestions was out of her control.

I awakened one morning barely able to get out of bed. The small of my back hurt so badly that I was in tears with every move. Somehow, I drove myself to a doctor's appointment and explained that I had been gardening for the last six days.

"How often are you taking breaks?" he asked accusingly.

"Oh, I stop for water breaks and of course, lunch," I replied. Never mind the lecture I got! He prescribed a muscle relaxer to relax my muscles and a narcotic pain reliever to help with the pain.

"Oh, and no more gardening until further notice," he exclaimed as I was leaving his office.

Great. Just great. Now, what would I do for distraction?

BLIND RAGE

The distraction came. Three days later I woke up with blurred vision in my right eye. I waited for it to pass but by 10:00 o'clock that morning, the blurriness was even more noticeable.

"Could you please relay this information to the doctor and have him call me as soon as possible?" I implored. "I'm really growing concerned. I think it must be the combination of medications he prescribed for me."

By 11:30 I was tired of waiting for him to return my call. I picked up the phone and called the pharmacist who had filled the prescriptions. The conversation was brief and quite unsettling.

"No, these medications wouldn't cause blurred vision when working individually or together," stated the pharmacist. "You'd better call your doctor right away. This time tell the receptionist that it's an emergency."

Now I was scared.

Barb left work and met me at the doctor's office thirty minutes later. It occurred to me on the way that I probably should not be driving a car, and I found myself praying the whole way to the office.

"Nancy, are you OK?" she asked as she rushed to my side with fear in her eyes.

"I don't know, Barb," I replied. "This is really weird. I see these little yellow dots marching out of the center line of vision in my right eye. It's blurry too. The left eye is fine."

"Marching yellow dots?" She frowned, looking confused.

"Marching, walking, dancing, I don't know" I declared emphatically. "I just know there's something really wrong with my eyesight. I'm so glad you're here."

I reached over to take her hand and felt her instinctively pull away as she glanced around the room. Seeing only an elderly gentleman snoozing in his chair, she reached back and took my hand in hers. This was, after all, no time to be concerned about someone's homophobia.

After examining my eye, the doctor didn't have a clue what was going on. He could see something in my eye, but he didn't know what it was. He asked his receptionist to set me up with an immediate appointment with an optometrist.

Leaving my Jeep at the doctor's office, Barb drove me to the appointment with a grave expression.

"Barb?" I asked.

"What, hon?"

"I'm really scared."

"I know," she said softly. "Me too."

The optometrist could definitely see something, but she didn't know what it was either. She dilated my eyes and spent considerable time looking, but it was unlike anything she had ever seen.

Although it was a Friday afternoon, she arranged an immediate emergency appointment with a nearby retina specialist.

"It's late in the day, but I called in a favor." She smiled.

"Thanks for all your help," I said, shakily. "I hope he can figure out what's going on."

"Dr. Paul is the best," she assured me. "You hang in there."

I will always be grateful to Dr. Paul for staying late that Friday afternoon. He, too, could see something, but it didn't make any sense to him. He said that if I had been thirty or forty years older my eye's condition might be more easily explained.

This had nothing to do with the pain medication or the muscle relaxer. This was a serious problem with my retina. I appeared to have very old scars in both of my eyes. Abnormal blood vessels had begun to develop and grow up through the scar in my right eye. It was rapidly taking out my vision. He had no idea what had caused the scars so many years ago, and he wasn't sure if he should try to laser surgery or wait. He chose to wait.

Within days my vision went from 20/20, with glasses, to 20/800 in my right eye. Over the next few weeks, the marching yellow dots, which I later learned were the actual retinal bleed, dried up and the eye began to repair itself as much as possible. I had, however, lost the central vision in the eye, and there was a good chance I would lose all of the vision in that eye within a month or so.

Dr. Paul sent me to a specialized retina clinic two hours away. The clinic was huge and intimidating. I had to chuckle, though, when a guy in the elevator smiled and said, "Hi, welcome to Retina World!"

I went through a battery of tests and was told that I had likely contracted histoplasmosis, a lung infection, as a child growing up on a farm. Left undetected, it had created scars in each of my eyes. For whatever reasons these abnormal blood vessels began to grow through the scar.

"I need you to know that you are likely going to lose all of the sight in your eye over time," said the doctor. "In fact, I am giving you a fifty-fifty chance of losing the sight in your other eye in much the same way. It could be tomorrow or it could be thirty years from now."

I didn't know what to say. I was frightened, tired, discouraged, lost in grief I barely recognized and going blind.

WOUNDED WARRIOR

I found this quote, attributed to Charles Swindoll, a Christian author, in Lowell D. Streiker's *An Encyclopedia of Humor*: "The church is the only outfit I know that shoots its wounded."

Ironically, while Mr. Streiker may have found this humorous, I found no humor, as I was indeed wounded. I found the simplest things to now be very difficult. I couldn't read easily. I had lost some depth perception and was unable to gauge distances. If I were in the dark, it was even more difficult. I was frightened much of the time.

My eye was patched, and I was aware of not only feeling different inside but also looking different on the outside. Hearing the rumor didn't help any. It seems that Lou, a member of the trustees, had been telling people in the church that they needed to find a way to get rid of me because if I lost the sight in the other eye they'd be stuck with a blind minister.

I thought this was the last straw, but I was wrong. When Lou came to talk with me about something unrelated, I decided to confront the matter head-on.

"Lou, this is difficult for me to talk about, but I recently heard that you have some concerns about me continuing to pastor here at Trinity," I said carefully.

"Well, I certainly do, Pastor," she asserted boldly. "With your eyesight being what it is and the chance of you losing sight in the other eye any day now, well I can't help but think it's time for you to consider moving on. We want what's best for the church now, don't we?"

I sat there in my chair dumbfounded. This was not a rumor. It was the truth.

"You know, Pastor," she continued, "when I was a young girl my parents told me that everything came from either God or the devil. I believe that this attack on your eye is from the devil. But here's the thing. Every time you tell someone that you've lost the sight in your eye, you are giving the devil glory. It's got to stop!"

"So, you want me to say what?" I asked incredulously.

"I want you to start telling people that your eye is one-hundred percent healed!" she exclaimed. "Give God the glory."

"But wouldn't that be a lie?" I asked.

"That doesn't matter," she exclaimed. "You just renounce the devil immediately and start telling people that God miraculously healed your eye. It's far better to lie and give God the glory than let the devil have his way."

When I got home that evening, I shared this conversation with Barb. She was horrified.

"How could someone say such a thing?"

"I don't know, but it's what Lou believes," I replied.

"So, are you going to start lying?"

I grinned. "Not just yet."

The good news was that Zach seemed to be adjusting to his new room. He was, at least, sleeping through the night, though he still preferred to play in the living room. Barb bought him a pirate's patch for his eye, and we spent an afternoon making pirate's hats out of the newspaper.

When she came out of the kitchen with a pirate's patch over her own eye, Zach giggled, "Now we're all pirates, not just Mama!"

A few days after Lou's visit another church member called to make an appointment with me.

"Pastor," Mattie began. "This is really hard to talk about, but I think I know why you lost the sight in your eye."

"Really?" I asked with interest.

"Yes, well, I think you obviously have some sin in your life you need to confess. Maybe something you did or said. Because you didn't confess it, God can't forgive you. I think God's trying to get your attention by punishing you."

"You think my loss of sight is God's punishment?" I asked with amazement.

"Yes. I don't want you mad at me, but I sure hope you'll confess soon so your vision will be restored. There are several of us who are starting a prayer group to pray for you about this."

I sat there dumbstruck as she got up, patted my shoulder, and walked out of my office.

"No way!" exclaimed Barb. "Mattie actually said that to you? I shudder to think who's in that prayer group."

"Me too," I replied. "I thought this was going to be such a great place for us, Barb. Now I'm beginning to wonder what I've gotten us into. Maybe we never should have left Grove City."

"Or the blue house?" She smiled.

"Or the blue house." I sighed.

The very next day a different member of the trustees dropped by my office to talk with me.

"Now this is hard to say, Pastor," began Patrick, "but since those scars were put in your eyes when you were a little girl, I suspect that there's something you did as a child that caused God to do so. Can you think back and remember anything you might have done to have upset God?"

"No, Patrick, I honestly can't think of anything I did to make God want to put scars in my eyes," I replied incredulously.

"I just want you to know that I'm praying for you to repent, Pastor. Once you've told the Lord how sorry you are, things will go a lot better for you."

"I didn't know what else to say," I told Barb that evening. "I never thought I'd hear those words out of Patrick's mouth."

"Oh, I could think of a lot of things you could have said," she retorted.

"I know. I thought of them too. But what good would it do? I just have to ride this thing through I guess."

"Hey, on a positive note, my sister called earlier today. No one died! She just called to chat."

"Now that *is* good news." I smiled.

OPERATING ON FUMES

The very next week the church organist stopped by my office after choir rehearsal.

"Pastor," she said tentatively. "I was wondering if I might have my husband stop by and put some sparkly tape along the edge of the chancel. I heard you've lost some depth perception. This might help so you don't stumble or fall. Gracious, we wouldn't want that on a Sunday morning, now, would we?"

Responding to her warmth and caring spirit I replied, "No, it wouldn't be pretty, would it? Thank you for your concern, Audrey."

As she was leaving, she turned and asked, "Oh, and by the way, do you think you could stop wearing that silly eye patch thing? It looks weird and makes the rest of us uncomfortable around you. Besides, we wouldn't want to frighten off our visitors, would we?"

Without waiting for a reply, she left, never realizing that back in my office I was sitting there sobbing into my hands.

I need to say, in all fairness, that there were some quietly supportive church members during this time. I know that there were those who lifted me up in prayer and offered to be of assistance if I needed them. I don't believe that most of the church ever knew about the theological rationales put upon me about my eyesight, or how this adverse theology affected me.

What I do know is that I found myself questioning God in ways I never had before. Was God punishing me? If so, what for? Was this the devil attacking me or simply a medical condition?

Because of the things that had been said to me by well-meaning people I was beginning to ask discerning questions. Was God punishing me for an unconfessed sin in my life? I didn't believe it in my heart of hearts, but waves of doubt rolled through my stomach in an acid-churned storm.

I was a pastor, and I had no answers to these questions. This made me feel even worse.

Choke....chug....sputter. Choke....chug...sputter. This is what had become of my spiritual life during that year and a half.

Where was God in the midst of all of this? Was God angry with me? Maybe I had taken a wrong turn. Perhaps I had been mistaken about coming to this church and this town. After all, things had been going wrong since right before we moved. Seventeen deaths in a year and a half, and the loss of vision in my eye had left me tired and frustrated.

I was a spiritual mess. I felt betrayed and abandoned by God. I was angry with life, angry with the church, angry with God, and angry with myself.

While I don't profess to be a psychologist, I do know now that I was depressed. How had I come to be in this situation? What could I, should I, have done differently to prevent it?

In the midst of my fiercest doubts though, I did not sense a call from God to resign my pulpit. But by then I was so frayed that I have to wonder if I would have recognized the call if it had come in over the telephone. I tried to listen to my heart to the best of my ability. My heart said that it wasn't time. I hadn't been at that church long enough to think about resigning. If I left so soon it would be nothing short of failure.

I was operating on fumes and knew that I desperately needed to be re-fueled if I were to survive. I began to focus on how I was going to fill up again spiritually. I began to lay out a survival plan.

My first step was to make an appointment with a grief-and-loss counselor.

"So have you decided who you're going to see?" Barb asked one evening as we sat on the floor watching *The Jungle Book* one more time.

"I've heard about a guy here in town who is okay dealing with gays and lesbians, so I'll check him out first."

"It irritates me that we can't just make appointments like other people do," Barb interjected. "First, we have to screen them to make sure they don't want to fix us or cure us of homosexuality before we can get down to the nitty-gritty of why we've come to see them."

"I know," I said with sadness. "It's hard to ask for help when what you get might cause you more harm in the long run. But I've talked with a couple of folks who claim he's good. If he starts in on my sexual orientation, I'll walk out."

"Okay, then. One more time through *The Bear Necessities,* and we'll get this little guy to bed."

I couldn't help but smile as the three of us held hands and sang with gusto!

I found myself on a three-week waiting list. I continued to plan despite this setback. Taking any kind of action brought me comfort.

Digging through my file cabinet one afternoon, I came upon my initial clergy-credentialing file. I pulled it out to read over for old time's sake. Something caught my eye. There it was. A requirement that my supervising pastor and I had agreed on during my student clergy years to keep me fresh and prevent burn-out:

I, Nancy, agree to go to Bear Head Lake State Park in Ely, Minnesota at least once a year during these two years I will be a student clergy. The purpose will be for rest, relaxation, renewal and spiritual retreat.

Bear Head! I'd forgotten about my camping trips to Ely. Maybe this was exactly what I needed at this time in my life: an escape to the north woods.

THE END OF THE ROAD

Ely, in St. Louis County of northeastern Minnesota, had its beginnings in the 1700s as a fur-trading post. It was incorporated as a town in 1888. After World War II most of the high-grade iron ore had been mined out throughout the United States and the search for low-grade iron ore was on. St. Louis County proved to be abundant with taconite, a very low-grade iron ore. The taconite was mined and reduced to pellets. It was then shipped to steel mills to be melted down into steel. As the steel mills began to slow down in production over time, the need for taconite slowed as well. Many of the townsfolk switched from life in the mines to tourism.

Today, Ely is a tiny town that sustains itself on those hearty folk from around the country who choose to pack and paddle into the Boundary Waters.

Ely is known as "The End of the Road" because it's located on the Boundary Waters that separate the United States and Canada. I've heard it said that you can only get beyond Ely by canoe, kayak, or dogsled.

I first discovered Bear Head Lake State Park in the early 1980s while searching for a "wild" tent-camping experience. Four and a half hours northeast of the Twin Cities of Minneapolis and St. Paul,

Minnesota, and twenty-something miles from Ely, the park is hidden deep in the pine woods sporting numerous lakes that provide some of the best fishing around. I would soon join loons, deer, wolves, eagles, moose, and of course, the bears.

It was here at Bear Head Lake that I first experienced *deafening silence*. Mountains are beautiful and the oceans are vast, but the northern woods of Ely, Minnesota are.... well.... SILENT. And very loud in their silence.

There was no doubt in my mind, I needed to pack my tent and camping gear and head to the woods. In so many ways I felt as though I was already at the end of the road or at least at the end of my rope. I decided that if I could get away for two weeks in these woods, I would come back to one of three things: the call to resign my pulpit, the call to resign my pulpit and my clergy credentials, or a new-found resurrection in my life and ministry. At this point, I had absolutely nothing to lose. The first step was getting this idea past Barb.

"Wait a minute," she said incredulously. "You want to go *where*?"

"I want to go to Bear Head Lake," I replied adamantly. "I used to go there every year, remember? It's where I found so much peace and serenity in my life."

"You used to go there when it was only five hours away," she chided me. "For crying out loud, Nancy, it would take you three days to get there! You've been cleared to drive, but you know how tired your eyes get. And what if you get all the way up there and something happens?"

"I can do it," I replied heatedly. "I'll just have to stop and rest my eyes every hour and a half or so. And what exactly do you think could happen up there?"

"You know exactly what I'm talking about," she said as her fears melted into tears streaming down her face.

"If I wake up blind in the other eye, I'll blow my whistle loudly." I was determined now. "A ranger will come and help me get to a telephone. Then you'll just have to come and get me."

There, the words had been spoken out loud. Her fears were on the table, and my practical response lay there beside them.

"Besides," I continued, "I've also realized that this might be the last time I see Bear Head." I didn't take this opportunity to share with her all the other things on that list of people, places and things I feared I'd never see again. "I'd like to refresh my mind in case something happens to my other eye."

"I can see there's no stopping you." Sadness filled her voice.

"I don't want you to look at it that way," I pleaded. "It's something I really need to do."

"Give me some time to wrap my head around it," she said quietly.

"Fair enough," I replied. In the back of my mind, I was already checking off the things I would need to bring with me. Where was my sleeping bag? And the tent, and .....

"Don't get too far ahead of yourself," Barb said with a tiny twinkle in her eyes. "I can already see the wheels spinning in your head. Do you really think you're going to get this by the church trustees?"

I had a sinking feeling in my stomach all of a sudden. How would they respond to my request for two weeks off to go to the woods in northern Minnesota?

I laid my cards on the table by telling them that seventeen deaths and the loss of sight in one eye had left me exhausted.

"I will either return to resign my pulpit, or I'll come back so refreshed and invigorated you won't recognize me."

Surprisingly, they unanimously agreed to give me the time away. In fact, they told me that if I needed to be gone for three weeks, that was OK with them. Perhaps I should have been wary of this generous response. But all I could think about was where I'd last seen my fishing pole.

I met with the grief-and-loss counselor once before I left for Bear Head Lake. He tried diligently to talk me out of the trip.

Puzzled, I asked him, "What exactly are you afraid of?"

He frowned, studied me a moment longer, then grumbled, "That you are planning on this being the end of you."

"Suicide?" I asked with a start. "You think I'll commit suicide there?"

He continued, "I think that your desire to go alone to a place so far away indicates there could be some danger" His eyes held mine.

I had to laugh. I didn't know how to explain to this man that I had no intention of hurting myself, only of finding myself, along with some healing along the way. I did my best to be convincing but left his office feeling much more at peace than he seemed to be.

The Sunday before I left, two women from my church asked to speak with me privately after worship. After previous private meetings with well-meaning members, I felt a bit gun shy. I knew them to be Native Americans, one of them from the Blackfeet tribe and the other a Cherokee.

"Pastor," said Allison Snow Owl, "we heard the church elders say that you are going to a sacred place where you will seek spiritual retreat. We have been worried about you. We've watched you over this past year, and we believe that the Great Spirit is about to do something very great in you during this time away."

Not sure of what to say, I merely smiled.

Margaret Raven Feather continued, "Pastor, we know that you are very conservative in your faith beliefs. We have a gift for you to take with you on your spiritual retreat, but we aren't sure how you will receive it."

Even more worried about their offering, I weakly smiled and grunted something I'm sure sounded less-than-excited. Allison reached forward with something in her closed hand. "Please hold out your hand," she said with a smile on her wrinkle-lined face. I did so rather reluctantly.

Margaret explained that they had made this small leather bag they were presenting to me. I smiled and nodded politely, not having a clue as to what they were talking about.

Margaret continued, "A medicine bag is where you will store treasures that remind you of your Creator and the Great Spirit's love for you. The things in this bag will bring you strength and courage. They will be medicine for you when you do not feel strong in spirit.

For now, we have each placed something from our own medicine bags into yours. Over time you will add your own things that will create your own personal medicine. Know too that things will come to or change out in your bag from time to time. This is hard to explain, but you will understand when it happens. Take with you the love of the Great Spirit and know that you have a sacred hand upon your head and your life."

With that they each smiled, hugged me, and left me holding the bag, so to speak.

What on earth was this thing? What was I supposed to do with it? It certainly wasn't Christian, and I wasn't too sure I should have taken it. Perhaps I was dabbling in something of the devil, after all. I didn't want to hurt these two well-meaning women, but I also didn't know that I wanted this *medicine bag.*

At the last minute, I packed it. It sort of drew me to it. I refused to wear it around my neck or carry it in my pocket, but I would take it with me. It made me uncomfortable yet, at the same time, it intrigued me.

BEAR HEAD LAKE STATE PARK

The magic began the moment I turned off Highway 169 onto the curvy wooded road that wound six or seven miles back to the park itself. As I came around the first curve, I hit my brakes hard. There, crossing the 2-lane road in front of me, stood a large doe with her tiny spotted fawn.

They paused in the middle of the road for a moment to take me in as I was taking them in. Then the deer scurried across the road and fled deep into the thick underbrush. Grinning, I drove on down the winding road and onto state park land. Rolling down the window, I breathed in the giant red pine, birch and maple enveloping me. I was here. I was really at Bear Head Lake State Park after all these years.

"Say now, it's been a while since we've seen you around here." The park ranger smiled. I recognized this lovely woman immediately. She and her husband had been Bear Head Lake State Park rangers for years! It was wonderful to see her familiar smiling face!

"It has been a while," I explained. "My family has moved twice since I was last here. We're now in the panhandle of Oklahoma."

"Goodness," she exclaimed. "And you decided to come here all by yourself to camp for a couple of weeks? You are a brave soul."

I shrugged. "Well, it's a long story, but plan on seeing me up here every few days to use the pay phone, outside. It's part of the bargain."

"You enjoy," she said. "And if you need anything, just stop by."

"Speaking of which," I replied, "I need some wood and some ice, please! I'm guessing I'll be back for more as the week goes on."

"We'll be here, she said with a smile.

After selecting a wooded campsite filled with towering trees, I began to set up camp. This was indeed a process as I unpacked the Jeep and organized the gear into the appropriate piles: food, tent, fire, fishing, and boat. Setting up the six-person tent was not an easy task with only one person doing all the work. It was, however, my first priority because I would have, if nothing else, shelter.

Once it was up, I placed the related gear inside: my backpack with clothing, sleeping bag, mat, pillow, and flashlight. I was glad I had taken so much time at home organizing everything. Although I was bound to discover that I'd forgotten something, I knew I had the basics.

Next, I moved the wood to a tree near the fire scar. I covered it with the blue tarp I'd brought along specifically for that purpose, knowing that although the sun was shining brightly at the moment, a Canadian storm could turn the weather nasty in a matter of minutes.

I paused to listen. Silence.

Soon I became aware of some birds in the distance. A huge raven flew overhead and landed on a tree branch as if to watch me. Seeing him perched there, I went to the food pile and pulled out some bread. I tore it into small pieces and threw it around the campsite and the surrounding underbrush. I knew better than to put out too much. I wanted the company of smaller creatures, but wasn't keen on attracting bears!

Next, I set up the cooler and the non-refrigerated food. The cast-iron frying pan found a spot on the seat of the heavy state park picnic table along with the other cookware. I pulled out the tripod-cooking grate and planted it firmly in the middle of the fire scar. It was all coming together, but suddenly I realized that the sweat coming to the surface of my skin was attracting all sorts of flying insects. I paused to cover myself with bug spray and sat down for a moment to enjoy the quiet, a diet cola in hand.

As I sat there, I slowly realized that I was feeling anxious. Looking at the tent, the woodpile, the fire scar and the food area, I felt secure in knowing I was doing the job correctly, but still, I was apprehensive. I was beginning to realize that soon I would have nothing more to do. It had taken me almost three hours to unload, organize and set up. Before long the kindling would be gathered, the wood split, the rest of the extra gear stowed in the Jeep, the food secured....and in that moment thunderous silence hit me.

It unsettled me, made me uneasy; I was so accustomed to the rat race of life, that I didn't know how to be alone with myself. I unconsciously decided that I would, at least on some level, fight it.

I got up and walked down to the lake. Seeing the boat ramp across the small bay I realized that I could use up time by launching the boat. Although I was tired from the three-day drive, I kept pushing myself. This was, after all, what I had been doing for the past year, pushing myself without ever allowing time for rest and relaxation.

I walked back to my campsite, hitched up the boat trailer to the Jeep, and drove down the narrow, dusty road that led to the small boat ramp. I hesitated, worried that someone would see how lousy I was at backing up the boat trailer, how slow and unsure I was at getting it in the water and off the trailer. As I pulled forward and began to back the Jeep and boat down the ramp, a pickup truck came around the bend pulling a boat.

I don't want to make these people wait was how I rationalized it to myself. But I knew that what I was really afraid of was them seeing my inadequacies. I pulled forward again, up and around the bend. I would wait for them to launch their boat first.

Getting out of the Jeep I watched from a distance as the people with the pickup truck launched their boat. I noticed that the two men seemed to be having some communication problems. The driver had to pull forward and try to back up straight several times before he got it right. Finally, he got the trailer down into the water while his friend worked to get the boat unhitched. Although he tried hard to stay dry,

I soon saw him slip off the trailer, standing in water that was a couple of feet deep. He cursed and laughed as the driver said something to him I couldn't hear. Soon the pick-up truck and trailer were parked, not far from me, and the two men were in the boat speeding across the bay.

I took a deep breath and started up the Jeep. I prayed that no one else would come until I was the one speeding across the bay. It didn't matter what I had just witnessed with these other folks. What mattered was that I wasn't seen making blunders.

No one else came and, after three tries, I had the boat and trailer backed down the boat ramp. I turned off the Jeep and came around to the trailer, now partially submerged in the crystal-clear water. I began to untie the boat and pushed it off the trailer. I took one, then two steps into the water to push it as far as I could. I was not in as deep as the last person in this spot, and I had a strange sense of satisfaction about that. I then tied the boat to the wooden dock and drove the Jeep and trailer up to the parking area.

"Please let the motor start. Please, God, let the motor start." This ran through my head over and over like a mantra as I suddenly realized how very tired, I was, not only from the drive and setting up camp, but from life itself.

I climbed into the boat and choked the motor while pumping up the gas bulb. I pulled the cord hard, but nothing happened. I pulled again and thought I might have heard something. Encouraged, I tried once more, and the motor tried to turn over. This time I pushed in the choke and pulled hard.

Vrrooom! It caught. With great pleasure, I heard the loud motor over the deafening quiet and saw the water swirling below. I untied the boat from the dock and settled down onto the boat seat. Pushing in the choke I turned the throttle and soon felt the warm wind blowing through my hair and dancing across my face as I headed across the small bay toward open water.

Shooting out across the main part of the lake was exhilarating. I saw the towering pine trees and the brilliant sun overhead. I felt a sense of peace I hadn't known for a long time. I pointed the bow out toward the wooded point.

Passing the swimming beach on my left, I began looking for the huge eagle's nest built high in the towering trees many years before. The angle wasn't right, but I wasn't concerned. I knew I would hike down to the beach another day to look for eagles. There were small pine trees everywhere as I plowed through the water along the shore.

Turning toward the left as I came around the swimming beach I remembered the time, years before when I had been walking through the woods in that very area. I remembered that I felt more than saw the Presence. It was a Holy Presence. Although I couldn't visualize it, somehow, I knew that it was filled with glowing light. I remembered that as this Presence came toward me, I had dropped to my knees, sensing the hand of something holy on my head.

It would be a long time before I told anyone that story.

I continued toward the east bay, watching the air for eagles and the water for loons. In a few hours, I'd come back out to the point to do some serious walleye fishing. For now, I decided to turn around, go back and tie up the boat on the side of the small bay closest to my campsite. I'd hike back down to the parking area later to get the Jeep.

SILENCE IS GOLDEN

Having been to Bear Head Lake periodically since the early 1980s, I knew that it would take me a good forty-eight hours to adjust to the silence and being alone. I knew the thrill I would l hold in my heart if the wind picked up and rustled the leaves. Ahhh, sacred sound; I was not alone.

Back at camp, a gray jay greeted me and waited for a hand-out. I pulled out a bag of old-fashioned animal crackers and dug through the ice in the cooler for a cold bottle of water. Settling into my camp chair I picked up a book I'd brought along and tried to read for a while. I couldn't seem to focus or concentrate, so I pulled out my camera and took some shots of the jay shoving crackers in his mouth.

Having been bit by the camera bug, I decided to hike the beach trail and go get the Jeep. I didn't see any great shots on the hike, but it was good to be walking through the woods. I drove back slowly watching for signs of wildlife, but nothing caught my eye.

Arriving back at the campsite once again, I pulled out the rest of my camera gear to clean the lenses. Then I checked the zippers on the tent, checked the ice in the cooler (again), and found myself thinking about what time I wanted to start supper.

Despite my busyness, I knew that darkness would eventually

come. It was inevitable. The sun would go down, and all I would know would be the snapping of the fire, the silence of the stars...and me.

I spent the late afternoon preparing the meal, not an easy task when one cooks real food over the open fire. This was a blessed event, however, as it gave me something to do. I dug through my cooler for the ingredients I needed. After chopping carrots, potatoes, and onions, I took out the raw hamburger and formed it into a large patty. Adding salt and pepper, I then placed the vegetables on top of the hamburger and encased it all in a wet paper towel. Lastly, it was all wrapped in aluminum foil. I placed the aluminum foil packet onto the hot red coals once they burned down to perfection. It took about twenty minutes for the meal to cook, ten minutes on each side. I ate the entire meal in about fifteen minutes

If I wanted to keep bears out of my food, I needed to make sure the clean-up was done well. Water needed to be heated over the remaining coals so I could wash the pans and dinnerware in my plastic tub, with biodegradable soap. I stored the leftover food in the cooler and tossed what I didn't want in the trash bag. After the dishes were washed and put away, I made sure all the food was safely secured in the Jeep. I wiped the door handles so that bears wouldn't smell food and try to break in. The garbage had to be carried down to the main dumpster in the park, and a new garbage bag was hung up. Over the next few days, this routine would become almost a sacred ritual.

I walked to the lake where I found the boat just as I'd left it, tied to a huge birch along the shore. I was looking forward to sitting out at the point fishing while watching a panoramic view of the setting sun.

Zipping out across the bay I spotted the point and headed directly for it. My mind eased back to the first time I learned about this fishing hole. I'd been camping at Bear Head Lake with a girlfriend. For three nights in a row, we'd arrived at the fish-cleaning house with one walleye and one northern pike, apiece. As we cleaned our fish, the door would open and in would come this guy with his three towheaded kids. Each one had their limit in walleye! We listened to the excited chatter of the children as their dad filleted the fish expertly. He occasionally glanced over at us and smiled, but never said a word. That is, until the third evening when I spoke up.

"Say there, I was wondering if you might give us a Fillet 101 lesson?" I asked hesitantly. "We don't seem to have as much meat left as you do."

"Sure," he said with obvious delight. "First of all, I never keep the Northerns. They have those awful Y bones that make filleting them a nightmare. The smaller ones are the best eating, but still hard to fillet. But I can sure help you with the walleye. Now that's my specialty." He grinned at us.

"My name's Keith," he offered. "These are my kids running around here with the fish heads." Again, he grinned as he shrugged his shoulders at his kid's idea of fun.

"I'm Nancy, and this is Jan," I told him. We don't seem to be having the fishing luck you guys are having."

After showing us how to slip the knife under the dorsal fin and slice downward at an angle, keeping the tail intact, he then opened up the side of the fish and demonstrated how to slice the meat all the way down to the tail.

"Now, do the other side," he commanded.

With newfound skill, I turned the fish over and began the same process. It worked!

"Now listen, ladies," he said with a smile, "tomorrow night you come out to the point across from the swimming beach and join me and the kids."

"Oh, we don't want to intrude on your fishing hole," began Jan.

"Nonsense," he added. "You'll be my guests. Not a minute after 7:30 if you want to experience all the fun. The first one always bites around 7:35."

With that he was out the door, rounding up his towheads, to hike back to their campsite.

"7:35?" Jan chortled as the door slammed behind him. "We'd better not be late, eh."

We arrived at the point by 7:15 the next night with great anticipation. Could this guy really deliver or was it just another fish story?

We weren't disappointed. As promised, the first fish hit Keith's line shortly after 7:30.

"Now just settle in and relax, ladies, because the fun will really begin in about thirty minutes."

As we sat there chatting with him, the kids gathered at the front of his boat and played Old Maid. Their lines were in the water and while I saw occasional glances, they seemed to understand it would be awhile until we got any action.

We learned that Keith was a pharmacist from St. Paul. He and his wife came every year with their kids. He explained that she didn't like to fish, so she stayed back at the campsite and had some downtime.

"You'll have to check out the pictures up at the ranger station," he said with pride. "There are several of our kids holding prize fish out of this lake."

Jan and I agreed to take a look the next time we stopped by the station.

"Dad, it's 8:05," stated one of the boys up in front.

"OK, folks, time to rock-n-roll," Keith replied with that ever-famous grin.

He placed a wad of tobacco in his cheek and began to chew. With a mysterious grin on his face, he pulled out a white floating jig-head and attached a black squirming leech, putting the number two hook right through the sucker of the leech.

"Ugh!" he exclaimed. "I hate leeches. But the Wally's love them."

He handed Jan and me each a jig head and the use of his leech locker. Grinning, he silently handed Jan a set of small pliers as he nodded toward the leeches.

Seeing her squirm he said, "OK, I'll put the first one on for each of you, but after that, you're on your own. With that, he spat tobacco juice into the water and said, "Now it's time."

We cast our lines toward shore almost in one giant motion. Instantly the lines went taut, and we began to pull in our prizes. By 9:30 it was beginning to get dark. We'd been so busy catching fish we hadn't even noticed the sunset.

We met Keith out there for two more nights, at his invitation, always catching our limit, then gathering in the fish house to clean them. But the third night he was quieter than usual as we hosed down the cleaning table.

"Ladies," Keith began hesitantly. "My wife has been a little concerned about me spending these evenings out on the lake with two women. I was wondering if the two of you would be willing to come back to our campsite tomorrow night after we fish? She just wants to meet you. She promises she'll have dessert waiting for us."

"Sure, Keith," we chimed together, giving each other a surprised look. It had never occurred to us that we might be the cause of marital discord.

"We'd love to meet your wife and put her mind at rest."

Again, we saw that grin.

"Thanks," he replied as he rounded up his kids and headed to his campsite.

"We never talked about us being lesbians," Jan said smiling. "I guess his poor wife must be nervous."

"I can't say I blame her," I added. "But Keith obviously has us figured out. He must believe that his wife will catch on quickly too."

Sure enough, the next night we met a very relieved-looking young woman.

"We must look really butch, eh?" Jan giggled later.

"I guess so," I said. But at least our fishing guide was off the hook.

We never saw Keith again, but every time I went up to Bear Head Lake after that, I checked the bulletin board for his blond-haired urchins. I was never disappointed. It was almost as if I got to watch them grow up through those photos.

. . .

Smiling at the memory, I arrived at the point, turned off the motor, and let the boat coast into position. Letting down the anchor, I turned to fix the line with a white floating jig-head and long squiggling leech. Soon after casting, I felt the distinct pull of a soft-mouthed walleye on my six-pound test. HIT! Time and time again I cast the line and felt the "player" nibble. I couldn't seem to set the hook no matter how many times I tried.

Just one more cast became my new mantra as I watched the sun go down behind the trees, first orange then red, and at last turning the sky a darkening gray-blue. I knew if I could wait and watch long enough, I might be blessed by the sight of an eagle gliding by. But for safety reasons, it was time to head back to shore.

I could smell wood burning from other campsites in the park as I came across the lake. The smell pleasing to my nose and reminded me that, although I was the only one in the whole lane where I had chosen to set up camp, I was not totally alone. I found myself wondering how successful I'd be in stirring up the earlier fire that had so graciously given of itself to cook my evening meal. And then, sooner than I wanted to be, I was tying up the boat and climbing up the steep bank toward the path that led to my campsite.

And there was the silence.

It was too early to go to bed and too dark to read. I was, at last, alone in the quiet with myself. I shuddered involuntarily. I tried to stay up until 10 o'clock. The time was filled with playing with the crackling campfire and picking up the lantern to check my watch. Finally, at 9:30 I could take no more. I gave myself permission to begin spreading out the coals and preparing for bed.

I lay awake in the tent for a long time. Silence. I couldn't even entertain a decent thought. In the distance, a wolf howled. This brought me no comfort. After a time, the haunting cry of a loon came over the water, magnified as the sound traveled through the trees. It was eerie and unsettling as I drifted off to a restless sleep.

SACRED PROCESS

I was awakened just before dawn by the joint efforts of my aching back and my screaming bladder. After struggling to throw on some clothes and my hiking boots, I stumbled out of the tent knowing that on this, my first full day here, a mental shift would begin to happen. I already knew that I would need to fight off the urge to drive the twenty miles into Ely or to go up to the ranger station to chat. But today I would not put on my watch. I would know where it was so that I could check it if I felt it necessary, but I wouldn't wear it.

As I began to put together the morning's fire, I chuckled at a chipmunk sitting on a rock next to the woodpile, his cheeks bulging with bread I had thrown out earlier. He seemed oblivious to me as he munched away happily. Soon I found myself anticipating one of my favorite camping games, Old One Match. The goal was to lay the perfect fire so that, with one lone match, I could get it blazing and then burned down to the perfect cooking coals. Hmmm. I must have been rusty because it took me four matches to get the fire going on this first morning.

I poured water into the tall metal cooking pot for coffee and placed it directly over the center of the fire. I sat down in my camping chair to feel the warmth of the fire. My knees were burning while my back was still cold. I stood for a little while with my back to the fire, but the warmth didn't seem to come up that high. Going back into the tent I pulled on my sweatshirt and felt a sense of comfort permeate my body.

Back in my chair, I noticed a small red squirrel sitting on top of the woodpile. He too was munching on bread. Grabbing the camera, I decided to play another game I enjoy in the woods. This one I call, "Let's Get the Perfect Picture." The red squirrel proved to be an excellent subject!

As the fire began to burn down into coals, the sun inched up over the trees. Although I couldn't see them, I could hear a variety of birds singing in the trees around the campsite. The distant cry of a loon over the water made me smile. I knew I would be looking for a great loon shot, the perfect loon shot before I left for home.

There was a soft hiss as the water began to boil. There's something special about camping coffee. I use a coffee process that turns ordinary ground coffee into a rich dark liquid. When that liquid is added to boiling water, the smoothest richest cup of coffee you've ever tasted is created. Even though I found myself picking stray ashes and an occasional bug out of my cup, the coffee was delicious.

The bacon was now crackling in the cast iron skillet. The eggs were ready to drop into the bacon grease, and I had toast slowly browning over to one side of the grate. It was a cholesterol nightmare but the perfect start to my first full day in the woods.

After breakfast I let the fire die down naturally. I had no idea what I was thinking about. I was just there in the presence of the moment. The sacred process was beginning to happen.

I'm so tired. This thought came to me out of the blue as I sat there in my camping chair drinking my third cup of coffee, watching the fire die out. Well, it's no wonder I was tired. I spent three days traveling, then four hours setting up camp, including getting the boat in the water. And then a restless night. Of course, I was tired.

Perhaps I'd stretch out in the tent a little later and take a snooze. That should refresh me. For the moment, I was content to sit there listening to the birds and watching the chipmunks and squirrels scurry around with bread in their mouths.

After I did the breakfast dishes and put everything away, I went into the tent to change into fresh clothes. Digging through my backpack searching for socks, I found a strange lump in one of the backpack pockets. Investigating a little more, I discovered the medicine bag. At the moment I wasn't sure what to do with it. I found myself somewhat frightened of the thing and was quickly reminded of my fundamentalist Christian roots. I knew in my heart that many Christians would tell me to throw the thing in the fire and be done with it. But it had been given to me out of love. I found myself intrigued by it, hoping at the same time that this wasn't some trick of the devil.

Taking the little leather bag out of the tent with me, I sat down in my chair and held it carefully in my hand as I sat by the fire that was now reduced to gray, smoldering ash. Deciding to investigate, I pulled at the draw string and slowly opened the bag.

Inside I found some sort of tooth, two animal claws from completely different animals (I didn't know *what* animals), some seeds, a greenish grayish dried plant-like substance, a couple of small stones, and what looked to be plain old dirt. Hmm. Interesting.

I decided it wouldn't hurt to carry the bag with me for the day, so I put everything back inside, pulled the drawstring tight and stuffed it unceremoniously into my pocket.

It was time to grab my camera and head out for a hike. Checking to be sure I had plenty of extra camera batteries, and film, I set off.

I took the dirt road to the boat landing, and then the heavily wooded path over to the swimming beach. I intended to hike the beach trail through the woods back to my campsite.

The sun was burning high overhead as I slowly walked down the narrow road. It was overgrown with vegetation, and I paused here and there to take a shot. I especially enjoyed using the macro zoom lens, shooting berries, flowers, old tree stumps and various fungi. My dream was to get some close-ups of wildlife. I had neither the photography training nor the huge lenses I needed, but the right moment just might come along. For this day I was content with shooting foliage and the occasional bee or butterfly. Every now and then I stopped to shoot the small gravel road behind me. It twisted and turned, weaving through the trees, reminding me of the road of life.

As I walked, I became aware of the wind moving gently through the leaves of the towering birch. I stopped to listen, hearing the hum of a distant boat motor out on the lake. The water seemed to be calling to me. After lunch, I'd head out in the boat. For now, I was at peace within myself as I walked slowly down the road.

Coming up the windy beach trail, I walked slowly and quietly. Surrounded by thick dense woods I found myself paying attention not only to the plentiful shades of green and brown but also to the dying and rotting tree stumps and logs. I paused again and again to shoot moss or some sort of fungus alive within the death of a rotting old stump.

I found myself thinking that I felt a lot like those stumps. It frightened me to think that way. I began to mentally list the deaths of those close to my heart in the past year and a half. Richard, Mick, Ken, Kelly, Larry, Darryl, Vickie, Brandon, Terry, Allie..... It's no wonder I felt I was dead and rotting inside. There had been so much loss.

Suddenly the woods seemed dark and foreboding. I could see the path in front of me, but something had definitely changed. With growing concern, I looked up at the sky and felt a profound sense of relief. Dark clouds surrounded me, and the sun was totally hidden. I realized that the darkness was literal darkness, and I almost laughed out loud with relief!

As I continued up the trail, I sensed that something deeper and darker was happening inside of me. I had pulled my head out of the sand, allowing myself a moment to feel some of the grief and loss that had been accumulating. I practically recoiled at all of the emotions buried deep within me.

Hurrying up the beach trail toward the campsite, I tucked my camera under my shirt as fat raindrops began to pelt me. Once I hit the clearing, I started running, thinking about how glad I was that I had covered the wood, zipped up the tent and tucked away my chair before setting out. I would slip into the tent and into some dry clothes and then wait out this summer shower.

In the distance, I heard thunder, and my heart jumped. In all the years I had camped, I had never grown accustomed to being in a tent during a storm. All the warnings about getting indoors and staying away from trees flashed across my mind. Here I was in the middle of the woods. What choices did I have?

Getting into dry clothes, I pulled a book and a flashlight out of my backpack. The thunder stayed in the distance, so my fear was quieting down. I did have a flash moment of wondering when was the last time I had waterproofed the tent.

Lying there reading, with a book in one hand and the flashlight in the other, I turned over onto my side. I felt a sharp jab in my upper leg. Digging into my pocket I pulled out the medicine bag I'd carried all day. Opening it I once again reviewed the objects inside. How could this possibly be medicine?

The thought came to me again, clear and persistent: *"I am so tired."*

It didn't surprise me. I'd hiked quite a way for my out-of-shape body, and all of the stooping and bending to get the right macro shots didn't help. Then I'd had to work a little harder coming up the rugged beach trail, and of course, there was the run back to camp in the rain. No wonder I was tired.

With the steady rain beating down on my tent, I turned off the flashlight and fell into a deep sleep.

LIFE, DEATH AND RESURRECTION

C hecking my watch for the third time that day, I was surprised to see that it was 4:30. I had been sleeping for two hours. The rain had stopped, but there were still dark clouds overhead with wispy gray streaks in the sky. Coming out of the tent, I dug through the cooler until I found an icy bottle of water. I drank until I felt revived.

The ground was wet, but the pine needles around the campsite had acted like mulch. There were no puddles, no mud, just wet sandy soil. I breathed in the scent of the wet woods. It had a musty smell with hints of pine and traces of something else I couldn't identify. No cosmetic company could ever capture that wonderful aroma, let alone bottle it.

I felt my senses awakened not only to the smells but also to the sounds and sights. There, to my left, caught up in the trees was a magnificent spider's web. If there hadn't been water droplets sparkling on it, I never would have seen it. It was beautiful, and I knew that despite my attempts and best intentions a photograph would never do it justice.

I also listened as the birds began to sing and chirp again. A chipmunk ran across the site, and I immediately pulled out a bag of cookies. Breaking them up, I threw them around the campsite as I had done earlier with the bread. I heard a small noise and saw the little red squirrel sitting up on the covered woodpile, looking at me as if to say, "C'mon now. Where's mine?"

I began to build a fire to restore the ash bed in the fire scar. Old One Match struck out again. It took me six matches to get the wood to light. Although it had been covered, it was still damp. I finally managed to get the dry kindling to catch with the help of a big strip of birch bark. Once the kindling caught, the larger pieces of wood began to catch.

As the fire roared to life a thought occurred to me. Here I was working to get a blazing fire, only so it could die down to create the hot coals I needed for cooking. I mentally struggled with this idea for a while, weaving in the concepts of life, death and resurrection. I knew that once the coals had done their job, I would hope for the near death of them while I went out to fish, then a total resurrection of the fire when I came back in off the lake, chilled from the cold.

Life, death, resurrection.

I pondered this for a while as I played with the fire. It occurred to me that you have to have life before death, and you have to have died before you experience resurrection. Since there is no earthly life that does not end, the three go hand in hand in a cycle of sorts. They didn't teach this in seminary.

This led to my thinking about why I was there at Bear Head Lake. How interesting that I had come to the "end of the road" in order to find myself. Would Ely be the end of the road for my professional ministry? Would it be a resurrection for my spirit? What if it became both?

The uneasy feeling returned. What if this didn't work? What if I left here knowing I had to resign my pulpit and my credentials? What would I do with my life then? I had worked so hard to come this far, and I knew that many clergies got into the field only to find themselves resigning within the first five years or so. I didn't want that to happen to me, but I also wanted God's will in my life and in the life of my church. Feeling anxious, I decided to finish my meal, clean up and go fishing.

We moved across the lake as one creature, this old boat and I. It was a fourteen-foot aluminum boat built in the mid-sixties. The 9.9 horsepower motor pushed us slow and steadily across the lake. I didn't open the motor too much. I just wanted to cruise slowly, taking in every detail of the shoreline. I found myself keeping a careful watch on the early evening sky as it looked like some more rain could be coming. The last thing I wanted was to be out on the lake during a storm.

I smiled when I again found that special spot out at the point. I dropped anchor knowing that on one side of me were the shallows where small crappie and sunnies would hit my line. On the other side of the boat was the drop-off where walleye congregated.

As Keith had taught me long ago, I started with a white floating jig head and added a feisty leach to the hook. Almost as soon as I cast, there was a distinct tug. I knew the importance of waiting for the right moment to set the hook. There is that distinct moment when you have to let the fish take the bait before you jerk on the line to embed the hook in the fish's mouth. Too soon and I'd lose the fish; too late and I'd lose the fish. I tried to set the hook but came up empty. The hook in the water now felt way too light so I slowly brought it up and found the leech was gone. I couldn't help but smile. I had lost a leech and some time, but I had a "player."

After a while I noticed dark clouds moving closer. I sighed as I pulled in my line. I'd had some good hits but nothing to show for it. I pulled in the leech locker, started up the motor and pulled up anchor. Soon I was nestled in my camp chair watching the fire dance in and out of the wood. Hearing distant thunder I said a little prayer for safety, and the thought came to me once again. *"I'm so tired."*

It began with sprinkles, but I knew the gentle rain would not likely continue that way. I covered the wood, put everything away and stowed my camp chair. I then headed down the lane toward the bathroom with running water and flush toilets, hoping I wouldn't need to return there, or the nearby outhouse, in the middle of a stormy night.

The rain continued throughout the night, and I awakened to something wet on my face. With surprise, I realized it was my pillow. The tent was leaking!

I had been so confident that the waterproofing was sufficient that I hadn't actually checked it. Bad decisions can lead to bad consequences. I moved my bedding away from the sides of the tent into the middle. Turning my pillow over I tried to go back to sleep. As the rain continued to steadily pound on the tent, I had a distinct feeling of doom.

It was the same feeling I'd had the day I was loading the moving truck and learned that our financing for the new house had fallen through. It was that feeling that somehow things were going to get much worse before they got better.

THE SHIFT

I awakened the next morning to the sound of tapping... no... drumming. There was no real beat to it, but it was definitely close by and very loud. I then realized that my bedding was wet, very wet! Ugh! Fortunately, my backpack was dry, so I had dry clothes. I lay there thinking about how much work this was going to be.

Listen.

There was that drumming noise again. I tried to quietly unzip the door to the tent, no easy task. Poking my head out I saw a drenched campsite. This time there were puddles. My body ached through and through as I struggled to pull on clothes and boots. I vowed that my next tent would be tall enough so that I could stand up in it. I also vowed to waterproof it.

Stepping out, I heard the drumming once again. There to my left, and overhead in a tree was a beautiful Hairy woodpecker the size of a robin. He was black and white with a spot of red on his head. His long bill was busy drilling into the tree as he moved up and down the branch in search of a breakfast of bugs. He ignored me as I trudged to the outhouse, thinking about the work that lay ahead. When I returned, I noticed him flying from tree to tree as I worked to get a fire started.

Forget the matches. I pulled out the lighter.

Some time and a lot of smoke later I had a fire going. My camping chair was damp and everything on me and around me felt wet. The good news was that the sun appeared to be coming up through the trees. Aha, resurrection!

"I'm so tired."

But how could I be tired? I'd just gotten up. Besides that, I hadn't even started the tough part yet. I needed to get the tent and bedding dried out and then head into town for some kind of waterproofing. The thought of all that work along with bailing out the boat and then getting a shower, so as to look presentable enough to go into town, exhausted me.

As the morning went on, though, the sun shone brighter than ever. I decided that was definitely a turn for the better. My attitude began to improve, and I soon found myself humming as I worked to dry everything off.

Much of the morning was spent draping things over the clothesline strung between two trees. When I ran out of line, I resorted to drying off the Jeep with an extra towel, and throwing wet things, like my sleeping bag, over the top of it. I also made breakfast, cleaned up, split more wood, and gathered some kindling to dry in the sun. After washing up, I sat for a while by the dying fire and thought about what I might use to bail the boat.

I soon gave up on the idea of driving into town for waterproofing. After all, the sun was out and things were definitely on the upswing. As my thoughts wandered, I pulled out my journal and began to write:

Thank You, God, for this glorious day. Thank you for the rain that washes the earth and reminds me to appreciate the sun. Thank you for some great fishing last night. I know I didn't catch anything but some great memories, but it was a wonderful time out on the lake. Thank you that the tent isn't any worse than it is and for the sun that is already drying everything out. Thank you that I am here in this sacred space. I love you and I am so very grateful. Amen.

As I finished writing this little prayer, I realized I couldn't remember the last time I'd felt grateful for anything. Yet here I was, grateful not only for the positive but also for the challenges. Something was definitely shifting inside of me. I couldn't believe how good it had felt to pray.

It occurred to me that, as a minister, I could say many prayers. Some of them had been really quite eloquent, some were memorized and rehearsed. But were they truly speaking to God from my heart?

I already knew the answer. I sat there wondering about the last intimate moment I'd had with God. As I wondered, I found myself getting up and grabbing another log to throw on the fire. This shift was just the beginning.

I had been taught that prayer is nothing more than talking to God, communicating with God. It occurred to me that when I wanted to talk to my mother, I simply picked up the telephone and dialed the number. There was intention on my part. In order to truly communicate I talked while she listened and then she responded while I listened. Was it possible for me to have a close, intimate relationship with someone I don't communicate with?

I went back in my mind to the sixth grade when I liked a boy, named Tommy, from another school. I knew his cousin, and she took messages back and forth between us. Things like, "I like you. Do you like me?" Tommy and I "went steady" for three months. I even had his ring, delivered to me via his cousin. We never spoke a single word to one another that whole time.

This is funny, right? But it's true! We claimed a steady relationship for three months, yet we never spoke one word to each other. Then, Tommy broke up with me. He had found another girl to wear his ring. It made me wonder if he ever spoke to her.

And I realized as I sat in front of the blazing fire, that my relationship with God was not unlike my relationship with Tommy. I believed in God, I loved God, I served God in my professional life, I studied about God. In essence, I was wearing God's ring. On some level, we communicated through the scriptures, hymns and religious readings. But the fact of the matter was that I did not have an intimate relationship with God.

Sitting there watching the coals slowly die out I began to feel as though I was in over my head. This was deep. How could my relationship with God be reduced to the same level as two sixth-grade kids?

Suddenly, I felt very tired and heavy. I couldn't lie down in the tent to rest because everything was wet. I was too tired to go and bail the boat. I just sat there feeling wiped out. I was running on empty. The warning light was coming on. Choke...chug...sputter.

As the coals evolved into ashes, I knew I couldn't sit there another moment. I decided to go for a walk with my camera. Perhaps if I kept my mind busy it would take away this discomfort.

I heard the woodpecker in the distance, drumming away. I headed down the road to the swimming beach hoping to catch some nice shots of raindrops coming off the foliage lining the narrow dirt road. I knew it was too wet to hike back into the woods on any of the deer trails or grassy paths, but I decided to take the beach trail back if it wasn't too wet and muddy. I sprayed on extra bug spray and set off.

As I trudged up the beach trail, I paused to shoot yet another picture of a rotting tree stump. Staring at it, I began to wonder if I was aiming for some sort of self-portrait. I felt a kinship with these old things, gutted and hollowed out, yet time and again I was surprised to find something new and alive growing inside.

Might there be something new and alive growing inside of me as well? I could only hope.

Seeing a tiny blue jay feather on the ground I stooped to pick it up. I looked at its brilliant colors and decided to add it to the medicine bag. After all, this was a beautiful feather, and the bag was supposed to be medicine for me. As I began to open the bag something caught my eye. I looked up to find a large doe crossing the path right in front of me.

I wasn't sure who was more startled! She paused as she looked at me. For an instant, I swear our eyes met; then she jumped and ran on across the path and into the dense thicket. I hurried up the trail to try to see where she'd gone, but it was too late.

If I hadn't been fooling around with putting the feather in that bag I might have had my camera ready. I'd missed a magnificent shot. Disgusted with myself, I finished putting the feather in the bag and had my camera in hand, ready for the next opportunity.

That night the tent was dry, and after some productive fishing, I sat by a cheery fire eating a dinner of walleye fried in cornmeal. I tucked into my sleeping bag around 10:30 and drifted off to sleep. It was my best night's sleep in a long, long time.

LOON LINE DANCING

The staccato tap of rain wakened me around 5:30 the next morning. Oh no, not again! The rain became more and more persistent. Within the next hour and a half, the rain beat on the tent until water started soaking through again. I got up, ran to the Jeep and flung open the doors. Throwing my sleeping gear and backpack into the backseat, I slipped into the roomier front seat. I was cold, wet, and downright miserable.

Driving to the shower house a short time later, I noticed that I was still the only camper in the whole lane. I took advantage of being the only person at the shower house and enjoyed the luxury of a long, soapy lukewarm shower. It felt great to wash off the multiple layers of bug spray and put on clean clothes.

I drove back to the campsite through the steady rain and made sure everything was as covered and protected as it could possibly be. And then I headed into Ely.

I was careful to watch for deer along the way, knowing they can be attracted to headlights during both dawn and dusk. It was still dark, but the rain was tapering off. This would be a great time to spot deer by the roadside and I wasn't disappointed. In fact, I slowed down considerably as I passed numbers five and six. The last thing I needed was a literal run-in with a deer or any other animal.

The Chocolate Moose in Ely was open just as I'd hoped it would be. This rustic log cabin restaurant is a wonderful place to eat. I remember when it first opened. They served blueberry pancakes using the blueberries they'd picked that very morning.

I ordered and enjoyed numerous cups of steaming hot coffee as I waited for my food and people-watched. Some of them were paddlers getting ready for a trip into Boundary Waters while others were just coming back. Some appeared to be tourists, and there was, in addition, an assortment of local shop owners I recognized from years past.

Sitting there I realized that it was a luxury to sit down in a restaurant and simply order a meal. Sitting in a restaurant is something I've done hundreds of times in my lifetime, and yet here I was thoroughly enjoying the fact that I hadn't had to gather kindling, lay the fire, light the fire, tend the fire, wait for it to turn to coals, prepare the food, dig out the cooking utensils, and on and on and on. I had taken a lot for granted before making this trip to the woods.

Although I felt a little guilty, I spent the better part of the day in town. I kept thinking that I should be back at the campsite gutting out the rain rather than languishing in the many comforts of town. Still, I shopped all the shops, purchasing souvenirs for my family and for myself. I bought some expensive paste to waterproof the tent, and a brush to paint it on with. I had lunch at Cranberry's restaurant, then drove out to both the International Wolf Center and the Dorothy Molter Museum. After reading Root Beer Lady about Dorothy Molter's life in the Boundary Waters Canoe Area, I knew I wanted to visit this museum to learn more. I was far from disappointed. The Wolf Center was fascinating, and I purchased a small stone from the gift shop that had the imprint of a wolf paw painted on it. I thought it might be a nice addition to the medicine bag.

What a glorious day! The sun was shining, and I knew that everything back at the campsite would be dried out. I headed back around 4:30 that afternoon feeling refreshed.

The storm rolled in around 6:00 that evening with a cannon volley of distant thunder. I was barely back at the campsite and trying to light a fire for supper when the first spatters fell. I couldn't imagine how much water must be in the boat waiting to be bailed. For the first time, I had the thought of giving up and going home, but for now, I needed to get things covered up again. I hopped into the Jeep as the lightning flashed and the thunder rolled. An hour later it was over, but the tent was too wet to waterproof. Sigh.

That evening, after bailing a couple of inches of water out of the boat, I was out at the point, a little late, but there, nonetheless. As I sat there waiting for a nibble, I noticed that the sun was once again out in its full brilliance.

It struck me that this trip, like life, was unpredictable. You had to take the good with the bad. Overall, it was good. Thinking about the loss of sight in my eye, I realized I hadn't given it much thought since I'd arrived at Bear Head Lake. I hadn't worn the patch since pulling into my campsite. I had been so busy, I forgot about my vision and the threat of going blind. I was also, unconsciously, finding ways to compensate. I found myself contrasting this with my life in my church. Overall, it was far from good. Overall, I felt like one huge failure. It was obvious that the leadership was not happy with me, and obvious that I was not happy with myself. Had I made a mistake in going there? Had I missed out on God's call somehow? Perhaps our signals had crossed.

Just then I noticed a loon land in the water about one hundred feet from me. If you've ever seen a loon land, you know it's comical. Once in the water, they are graceful and beautiful creatures, but they land in the water awkwardly with a splash and a long slide. I watched for a while then felt another small crappie take the bait.

As I was releasing it, another loon swooped in and did its crash landing into the lake. I saw that the first one was still in the vicinity as only a few minutes had gone by. Splash! There was another one! And another.... As I sat there releasing back small crappie and perch, twelve loons flew in and did their crash-landing into the lake. Being in what was apparently the only boat out on the lake that night, I was in for quite a show.

Now one might think I'd lost my mind, but it really happened. Those loons formed what appeared to be two lines and did the closest thing to a dance I have ever seen animals in the wild perform. They moved, almost as a unit, with flapping wings and loud cries. The two lines would move toward each other and then back up again as if on cue.

Pulling in my line so as to not be disturbed by small fish, I sat watching, mesmerized. Oh, what I'd have given for a video camera! I watched this dance for three-quarters of an hour. Then, almost as if by some silent signal, they began to fly off, one at a time, in different directions until not a loon was left. I would not have believed it if I hadn't seen it.

Checking in at the ranger's station the next day I was embarrassed to learn that no one had a clue what I was talking about. They knew nothing about any "loon line dancing." Now I was the one who felt loony; but I knew that I had indeed witnessed something very special, and in some way very sacred.

IN MEMORY

I spent much of the next morning painting my tent with the waterproof paste. I was glad that I had bought so much of it because I wanted to be sure to cover the whole tent with a nice even coating. I prayed it would have time to dry and set before the next rain came.

Later that afternoon I realized I was feeling sad and heavy inside. It was new for me to be aware of my feelings and I wasn't too sure how I *felt* about it, pun intended. I picked up my much-neglected journal and found myself writing, *I'm so tired. Too much loss.*

It was all I wrote before hot tears sprang to my eyes. Getting up to find a tissue, I noticed some small stones in the campsite. They had been there all along, but I hadn't really noticed them until this moment. An idea came to me. Retrieving a fine-line marker from my backpack, I laid it on my journal and began to pick up various stones that were now catching my eye. Once I had twenty of them, I sat down and held them in my hand, one at a time.

Not sure where I was going with this, I found myself selecting one stone for my dog, Allie, and one for each of the people who had died. I also chose one for the loss of sight in my eye, one for Toby the cat we'd left behind, and one for all the pain involved in that move. Using the marker, I wrote a name or subject on each one.

Then I took each stone, one at a time, and held it in my hand as I held that person or situation in my heart. I had a time of remembrance for each one, then I prayed for God's help to let them go. When I felt ready, I threw each stone, as far as I could, into the woods behind the campsite, in every direction. When all the stones were gone, I felt remarkably lighter in my spirit.

I'd be dishonest if I told you that it was easy for me to throw those stones. I held each one close to my heart and experienced memory after memory of that person or situation. I prayed, remembered, and shed tears. Some were harder to throw than others. I struggled with the concept of "throwing them away" as opposed to "throwing them away from me" because discarding them seemed disrespectful to their memory. I also knew that I needed to have the memory and the pain, then let go.

I hadn't attended the funerals of these people. I hadn't had the opportunity to know the healthy grieving, then the healthy letting go. In retrospect, I held at least seventeen small memorial services that day. When I looked at the sun in the sky, I knew that some significant time had gone by. Can you imagine my surprise when I checked my watch, in the tent, and realized it had been over three hours?

I felt energized and exhausted all at the same time. Unsure of what to do, as I was too tired to hike, build a fire or take the boat out, and too filled with energy to take a nap, I pulled out my journal and began to write:

Most Loving God, I thank you for every life represented in this ritual today. Thank you for those who have gone on to be with you. I am so grateful for each and every life and for the ways in which they touched my life. Thank you for my family back at home, my family in Pennsylvania, and my family in Minnesota. Thank you for my church family, not only for the joy they bring to my life but also for the challenges they bring. I am beginning to understand that these tough times are challenging me to work and become stronger. As I sit here sunburned, muscles aching and sore, I realize

that I have become stronger in these past days. I realize that along with the good in life, there are also the things that challenge me. I realize that while the good is a blessing, the challenges can bring growth. What a concept, God! I am sitting here thanking you for the tough times that are making me a stronger and healthier person; physically, mentally, emotionally, and spiritually. I know it sounds strange, God, but sitting here right now I want to thank you for the rain. Thank you for the loss of sight in this eye (though I'm not saying you or I caused it). Thank you for the loss of seventeen people and my precious dog, Allie. Thank you for the stresses involved in our family move. Although I'm not sure I believe you cause or allow such things to happen, I do believe that you work through all circumstances and I believe that through it all, you are working good work in my life right now. I also want to thank you for the woods. Thank you for the trees, with all their varieties, and yet similarities. Thank you for the birds and the fish and the chips and squirrels. Thank you for the bear, wolves, moose, deer, and other animals that live here. Thank you for the loons and their chilling sounds over the lake, for the eagles and wood ducks and other animals here. Thank you for the berries and fungi and insects that land on them for food. And though I'm not ready to thank you for the mosquitos and wood ticks, I do thank you for the leeches that help me to catch fish. And thank you for the water and the life therein, and the sky and the life therein. Thank you
for my life, God
Amen

I was becoming a new creature. I am still amazed that I had come to this place in just a matter of days.

As I set off for the lake, I had the distinct sense that I was going spiritually deeper. Walking down a deer path I saw a tiny stone at my feet. I can't tell you why it seemed to call to me, but it did. I stooped to pick it up and placed it into my medicine bag with the small feather and objects from the two Indian women.

Can you imagine my surprise when I realized the feather was gone? It had simply vanished from this tightly closed pouch. I hadn't opened the pouch since the day I put the feather in it; there was really no explanation. But I remembered the women saying,

"Sometimes things come and go in our medicine bags; it's just what is." I hadn't really understood what they were talking about, but suddenly it occurred to me that the work I'd done that afternoon had so lifted my spirit that it was almost as if the heaviness inside of me had simply flown away. Perhaps with the help of that feather?

Oh, now this was getting ridiculous! What was I thinking? How could a feather in a leather pouch simply disappear as if to symbolize the lifting and flying away of a substantial amount of my grieving? There was nothing about this in the Bible! And yet it came to me, "I will raise you up on eagle's wings." The thought brought warmth and comfort to me. The feather was gone and for me, it symbolically represented the flying away of some of my grief. The one tiny stone was now there to represent the seventeen deaths I had released. And although a stone is heavier than a feather, somehow my load felt altogether lighter.

TABLE DANCING WITH THE STARS

That night I skipped fishing; I was just too tired. I sat down by the lake for over an hour pondering the afternoon's experiences, before heading back to camp to build a fire for a late supper. I wanted to be sure to have everything cleaned up before nightfall.

While waiting for the coals to burn down I opened my journal and wrote:

God, I am so tired.

Before I could think another thought, I heard a voice inside of my head responding: *Well, are you really surprised?*

I was more surprised at the reply than at being so tired! A dialogue seemed to be taking place and while a part of me felt uneasy, another part of me determined to journal it word for word.

Me: What do you mean?

Voice: Well, you've been through a great deal of trauma. You have been affected physically, emotionally, mentally, and spiritually.

Me: Was I wrong to have come here?

Voice: Why would healing be wrong? Sometimes you have to be away from your life in order to do the work you need to do. But it is difficult work,nonetheless. Adding to the mental, emotional, and spiritual work you are doing, the physical aspect of this trip is also tiring.

Me: There is a lot of physical work involved here, isn't there? But somehow, it's healing for me. I like this kind of work.

Voice: Because?

Me: Because it's basic survival. I have priorities in place and if I tend to them faithfully, things go pretty well. For example, if I don't have shelter, I'm in trouble. If I don't chop wood and gather kindling, there's no fire for warmth and no food.

Voice: So you enjoy doing this kind of work because there's a plan in place that insures your survival?

Me: Yes! Does that make sense?

Voice: Do you feel like you have more control over your life here?

At that moment it hit me. Back home, I felt as though I could not survive all the grief and loss I had encountered. Here I could do something that assured my physical survival. I felt, indeed, that I had more control over my life here in the woods. Even against the elements of nature, I felt more at home and at ease here than I did back in the "real world."

I thought about this for a long time as I watched the wood burn down to ashes.

I was in my sleeping bag by 10:00 o'clock, tired from the emotions of the day. I fell into a deep sleep with the medicine bag placed close beside my glasses, car keys and wallet. It now seemed natural to include the medicine bag with my other important belongings.

Somewhere along the way, I had taken ownership of it. Or had it taken ownership of me?

I was not pleased to have my bladder awaken me sharply from a deep sleep several hours later. I tried to ignore it, turning to this position and that, but it was of no use. Turning on the flashlight I checked my watch: 2:00 o'clock. I pulled on a pair of shorts, my boots and a t-shirt and slid out of the tent. I gasped in wonder as I glanced up to see millions of huge glowing stars overhead. They were so low and so immense it seemed as though I could reach up and touch them. It was absolutely amazing! I had never before seen such a sky!

After taking care of the bodily demand at the outhouse, I sat down on the top of the picnic table, marveling at the celestial display. A few moments later, laughing out loud, I climbed up onto the table and stood there, very childlike, reaching up into the heavens, trying to see if I could touch them. Of course, I couldn't reach even one star but found a sense of delight inside that I had even tried. Taking a few steps forward and then a few back in reckless abandon, I imagined myself waltzing there on the top of that picnic table to music that was heavenly, and playing loudly, all in my head.

It was after 3:00 o'clock when I crawled back into the tent and fell asleep with a huge grin pasted on my face. I had witnessed an awesome heavenly display!

Perhaps more importantly I had been able to see something very good come out of something very irritating. If my bladder hadn't awakened me, I would have missed the whole thing! Perhaps it was time to keep a closer eye on what I could learn from the irksome times, those times I have absolutely no control over.

A SINKING FEELING

I had now been in the woods for seven days. I called home every three to four days, as I knew Barb was concerned about my being so far away and alone. As I put in a phone call to her that day, I assured her that my eyes hadn't changed or gotten any worse, and that, although it must seem to her like I was all alone, I truly felt God's presence with me.

It was easy to tell her about the fishing and the rain and the trip into town. It was harder to describe what was happening inside of me. I didn't try, and I knew she could sense that I wasn't telling her everything. Respecting my process and journey, she was quick to let me know that she loved me and was holding me up in her prayers.

But then she asked, "How much longer, Nanc?"

I was ready for the question. "One more week, I think."

I knew that despite the hard work, the rain, my aching back and sunburned skin, I was getting some very important spiritual lessons here in the woods. I wasn't ready to try to explain this, and I was grateful she didn't press me. Smiling to myself as I walked back toward my campsite I thought, *one more week will either cure me or kill me.*

That afternoon I decided to take a long afternoon boat ride to explore every nook and cranny of Bear Head Lake. I packed a light lunch with fruit, veggies and trail mix, filled the canteen with water, and put my camera into a large waterproof bag. The motor started without hesitation, and I zoomed toward the back bay. Feeling the wind on my face was simply glorious. I pulled my wide-brimmed hat down a little lower to protect my eyes from the bright sunlight.

As I came along the shoreline, I watched for wildlife. Soon, I spotted a brown beaver swimming toward a large beaver dam. I marveled at their structural ingenuity as I zipped past the beaver. Beyond the dam, I came to another part of the lake but hesitated to put the boat into that little cove. I had a memory of some years back when I had been with a friend canoeing on this part of the lake. We had been surprised at how shallow it was. When we put our paddles down into the lake, we discovered that it had a false bottom. What appeared to be the bottom of the lake was simply a build-up of silt and sand and such. I cannot tell you, geologically, what creates a false bottom in a lake. I knew that it was cause for reflection. How could something look so real and yet be so fake?

I felt myself shiver involuntarily. I knew that this was a physical response to a deeply spiritual issue. Not wanting to think about it just yet, I revved the motor and headed toward another part of the lake.

Twenty minutes later I was sitting in the boat, in the middle of the lake, across from the swimming beach. I could hear the voices of people splashing in the lake and picnicking there on the grounds. I figured this must be the communal gathering place because I hadn't seen people all week. I noticed that the depth finder read just over forty feet. I hadn't realized the lake was so deep! Suddenly I felt uneasy. I still had my life jacket on, and the boat was the same one I'd used for years. But now I had a difficult time, knowing that the water was so deep.

Deep things seemed to frighten me.

I realized I didn't want to sit there and have my lunch after all. I decided to start the motor and move to a more comfortable spot. When I turned around the unthinkable happened; my foot kicked out the boat plug!

I knew that this particular plug hadn't been designed for my boat, but I'd lost the metal screw-in plug during the move to our new home. I'd purchased this plug and pushed it in as far as I could, but an edge still stuck out. This edge was what I'd struck with my foot.

I cannot describe the panic I felt as lake water began to gush in and fill the bottom of the boat. I honestly didn't know what to do. I pictured the boat sinking below me and instinctively tightened the straps on my lifejacket. I spotted the plastic container I'd been using to bail water out of the boat since the rains, but I knew this wasn't a viable option.

I yelled, "God help me!"

In the midst of absolute chaos, I heard the steady voice in my mind I was coming to recognize and trust: *Start the engine and run the boat into the swimming beach.* There was no time to argue or question.

The motor started on the first pull, and I watched with astonishment as the water on the floor of the boat began to rush back out of the small hole where the plug had been. It was full speed ahead as I pointed the boat toward the beach.

There were children swimming and I quickly remembered the dock around the side of the beach. If this boat was going to sink, it was going to sink in as shallow water as I could find.

The kids must have seen that I wasn't slowing down. Perhaps they saw the panic in my eyes. Two of them came splashing through the waist-deep water, toward the boat, yelling, "What's wrong?"

I yelled back, "I kicked out the boat plug!!" I cut the motor and was moving rapidly up to the dock when the kids rounded the bend.

The younger one, around eleven years old, yelled, "Show me where the plug goes."

I pointed and like the little Dutch child who saved the town by putting his finger in the dike, he smiled at me as he calmly pushed his finger into the hole stopping the flow of water.

"Now bail her out," he commanded as the older boy yelled, "I'll get Dad."

I felt like an idiot sitting there in the boat bailing it out, when three grown men and their wives came running. "You say you've kicked out the boat plug?" asked a blond Minnesotan with a thick Iron Range accent.

"Yes, I don't have a plug that fits well...and...." I was replying when he cut me off asking, "Where is the plug?"

I gave him the plug. He handed it to his son, the boy with his finger still in the hole. "Give 'er a try," he said. The child couldn't get the plug to fit no matter how hard he tried. The man said, "Well, give 'er to me. It was in there once and it will go in again. Now let me think...."

"Butter," said the other guy.

"Hmm?" the first one asked.

"Butter. We can grease 'er with butter and slide 'er in good and tight."

And that's exactly what they did! One of the boys ran the plug back to the picnic area where they'd been having lunch. Thank God they had some butter (or margarine, I didn't ask) and greased that plug like a pig. I moved forward as the men gathered in the back of the boat and slipped that boat plug in so that not even an eighth of an inch was sticking out. It was a perfect fit.

Looking at me the man said, "And if I were you, I'd never take that plug out again." They all laughed heartily. As I yelled my heartfelt gratitude they were already disappearing behind the trees.

I found myself caught between feeling like an absolute fool while feeling some of the most intense gratitude I'd ever experienced. Having lost my appetite, I decided to not have my picnic lunch. Instead, I headed back to the campsite. I needed to feel my land legs again with all the security that comes with them.

My hands were shaking and my mind racing as I maneuvered the boat between some jumbled logs at the bottom of the lake. I wasn't being as cautious as I should have been. I quickly and recklessly cut the motor, jumped out of the boat and tied it up to the nearest tree. There would be a price to pay for my carelessness.

FALSE BOTTOM THEOLOGY

A s I sat at my campsite eating lunch, I thought about the events of the day. My hands were still shaking as I bit into an apple. A horrific picture ran through my mind, as if I were watching a video replay. *There I was in forty feet of water and the boat was already filling rapidly and beginning to sink.* STOP. FAST FORWARD. *The men are putting the well-greased plug into the boat, and everything is OK.* But what if it hadn't turned out OK?

I pulled out my journal and wrote the word that blazed through my mind. TRUST.

I gazed at it for a long time. Part of me wanted to go deeper and another part of me was screaming to run away from this word with all its baggage. This is a word that has not held much meaning for me over the past thirty-something years. I didn't really experience it as a child or as an adolescent. I certainly wasn't familiar with it as an adult.

Whom did I trust? I quickly wrote down the word: *God*. Of course, I trusted God. After all, I was a pastor who had been called by God to do God's work.

But did I really and truly trust God? Sitting there in the middle of the woods I found myself writing something very shocking. There in my journal I wrote: *"No. I do not trust God."* I waited. Nothing happened.

I looked up, sure that lightning would soon strike the nearest tree which would topple into my campsite and squash me like a bug. The sky was clear with a thin layer of wispy clouds. The sun was out. There was no lightning, no squashing. And it occurred to me: What *was* my image of God? Why was I so afraid to honestly admit I didn't trust God?

I found myself writing frantically. My pen could hardly keep up with my mind as the words flowed through my brain and into my hand that wrote with a passion.

Where was God when I was a child? Where was God when all those different people abused me as a child? Where was God when all the violence and threats of violence erupted within our home? Where was God when my mother wept, and my father raged as my brother's addiction to alcohol led our family spiraling downward in grief, fear and despair?

I couldn't seem to stop. The words rolled out of my pen almost as if they had taken on a life of their own.

Where was God when I was a young woman caught up in the fear and ignorance surrounding my sexual orientation? Where was God when those people told me I was sick, but that God loved me and would heal me from homosexuality? Where was God when some of those same well-meaning people held me down in a chair, screaming at me for the demons of homosexuality to come out of me? Where was God when they ranted until my head throbbed and my body ached from their harsh holding? And where was God when I lay awake night after night sobbing into my pillow, believing that God must not love me because I was still a lesbian?

Continuing to write fast and furious:

Where was God when the house we were to move into became unavailable? When we had to leave Toby behind? How do I trust in a God who could allow our little son to feel such pain and loss only because his mama was trying to be obedient? Where was God when all those people I held dear died within a year and a half? How could we be hit again and again and again with the news of yet another death? And what was God thinking when I realized I was going blind in one eye? How was I to trust a God who used such pain to teach me a lesson, or punished me, when I didn't even know what I had done to deserve this? What kind of parent treats their children that way?

My journal was wet. I could see the words smear as drops of water landed on my writing, creating a mess. That's how I felt, a smeared, jumbled mess.

I soon realized that it wasn't raining. I was crying. Tears were pouring down my face and falling onto my writing almost as if trying to wash it all away. But I would not allow it to be washed away. I would not allow this rage I felt to simply vanish along with the smeared words. It had taken me a lifetime to feel this angry with God, and I wasn't going to let go of it....at least not yet.

I awakened after a two-hour nap feeling as though I'd been in a wrestling match and lost. My head was throbbing, my sinuses screaming, and I ached all over. Coming out of the tent I drank some cold water and sat in my camping chair for a while. Then I had a realization.

My spiritual life had been like that false bottom in the lake; shallow, with a special covering over the deep places. Oh, from a distance it looked just like the rest of the lake. But if you were upon it, you could see how very shallow it was. And if you truly began poking around in it you would soon discover that the bottom was fake.

I reached for my journal and opening it up once again, began to write:

My spirit sits here sheltered in this sanctuary of the woods knowing that God is here. And the water? What does the water represent? My longings? My life? My future? My destiny? My desires? It is so much more than the surface. The sparkles on the water bid me to come and play, and I so want to be upon it. Yet a part of me fears the deep. I must go into it; or not. I cannot see the lake from where I sit, but I only need to walk a short distance and there I will see the sparkles of sunlight dancing on the surface. I watch the water dance with the shoreline, and a part of me wants badly to go and dance with them. I don't believe I can. I don't want to believe there might be a place for me. I come closer to the water, and I feel the sun on my shoulders. The sun is my encouragement, my affirmation. The sun represents love for me. It bids me to come, to take my place and enter into the dance. I do not see myself belonging there. I cannot dance on the water. I can only go INTO the water...and it is deep and there is much that lurks there unknown. There are things there that I may not want to have touch me. There are bloodsucking leeches. I know they are there because I let them go after a season. They will attach to me. They may suck the life out of me. In the depths of the waters are my fears. They run very deep. It is my fears that keep me from the dance. I am suddenly very tired. I don't want to write anymore right now.

Reflecting back on this journal entry I saw I did want to go deeper, but it was a lot more painful than I'd ever dreamed it would be. Interestingly enough, at this place in time, I had no thoughts of packing up and going home. I knew that something had begun that needed to see itself through to an end. I just didn't know what end.

As I prepared the fire for the evening's meal, I had a moment of glory as Old One Match prevailed for the first time on this entire trip. I decided that some comfort food might be appropriate and began to prepare a foil dinner.

I wasn't too sure how things stood with God at the moment. I was trying to avoid God, but it seemed that in everything I did, I kept bumping into God, as if God wanted my attention to tell me something, but I couldn't bring myself to listen. I just didn't trust that God would have anything nice to say to me after I ranted and raved in my journal, earlier in the day. And now I realized the depth of my fears. I felt guilty, but I didn't feel sorry. Not one bit.

As I finished preparing the foil dinner, I placed it on the hot coals and sat down to wait while the meat, potatoes, carrots and onions cooked. I had an assortment of visitors while I waited. Several chipmunks showed up, and the little red squirrel came to play around the woodpile. Some other kind of squirrel-like creature came into the site. I later learned it was a species of ground squirrel. I didn't really care. I just put out a little extra bread and animal crackers.

A little while later I noticed several birds swooping down to have some treats as well. It was a lively campsite, and I reached for my camera to snap a few shots as I listened to the hiss and snap of the food beginning to cook within the foil. The growl of my stomach reminded me that I hadn't eaten lunch. I knew better than to try to rush the meal, however. Some things must simply take their time. Cooking over an open fire is one of them; processing my relationship with God was another.

That evening I set out to do some fishing. Feeling more secure about the boat plug than I had since losing the screw-in metal one, I had the tiniest moment of relief. It occurred to me that because something awful had happened, something very good had happened. I was allowing myself to ponder this as I climbed into the boat and realized that the motor was stuck on a log.

Because I had not been careful when I brought it to shore earlier in the day, the boat had floated out and over the top of a downed tree in the water. The propeller appeared to have dug into the log. I tried everything, then finally gave up and got into the hip-deep water.

Trying to dislodge the propeller from the tree, I grabbed onto the boat to balance myself. I felt a sharp jab into my knee and saw the water turn red. Looking up, I realized that I had carelessly grabbed hold of the handle of the trolling motor for balance rather than the boat. Quite by accident, I'd turned on the electric trolling motor. The propeller had ripped into my knee. I quickly turned it off just as the prop from the motor came free from the log.

It didn't really matter anymore. I climbed up out of the water and took a look at the gash in my knee. Not sure if I needed stitches, I limped up the hill and back to my campsite.

Pulling out the first aid kit I was able to patch up the gash without a problem. There was no need for stitches. The cut wasn't deep, just wide. I bandaged it carefully and took an over-the-counter pain reliever.

Settling back into my camping chair I felt beat. Whipped. Done in. I felt as though I had wrestled with God all afternoon and now, like Jacob of the Old Testament, I too was walking with a limp.

Was this God's punishment, or simply something that had happened by accident? I found myself wondering the same thing about the boat plug. Was it some sort of punishment by God or simply something that had happened?

Then my mind turned to my eye, the seventeen deaths, the tension in my church. Where WAS God in the midst of all of this? And how was I to trust God when I never knew if I was going to be blessed or blindsided? No wonder I'd stayed with a false-bottom theology. It didn't require me to think or feel.

RETREAT

I t won't surprise you to learn that it rained that night. It started around midnight, by my internal clock. It rained far into the morning, and I ached all over. The waterproofing seemed to hold on to the tent—hallelujah—but the campsite was drenched again.

I said the words quietly as I rose from my sleeping bag, my knee throbbing. "God help me."

I really can't explain what happened next as it came about so suddenly. Standing there, looking at the puddles in that soaking wet campsite, I got angry. Very angry. I had this incredible urge to fight, but fight what? Fight the meteorologist? Fight the rain clouds? Fight God? I didn't know.

Without thought, I began to take drastic action! Throwing my backpack and book bag into the back of the Jeep, I checked the campsite to be sure the wood was covered and everything else as secured as possible. I brought the cooler and all the food with me, as well as my sleeping bag and pillow. I jumped in and started the engine as a crack of thunder broke the morning silence. I didn't want to go home yet, but I knew I had to have a break.

As I was driving the seven miles, down the dirt road, to the main highway a big old bear crossed the road right in front of the Jeep. I slowed down and it stopped and looked at me for a moment. Then it snorted and lumbered on across the road. I had seen my first bear outside of a zoo. How could I feel so lousy and yet so exhilarated at the same time?

Walking into the lobby of an Ely hotel, I knew that I looked bad and probably smelled worse. The desk clerk smiled and asked, "Just coming in from the boundary waters?"

"No, the state park," I responded, just daring her to assume people who stay in the park are wimpier than those who venture out into the Boundary Waters Canoe Area.

Sensing something from within me, she simply smiled and said, "Rotten weather, isn't it? How long will you be staying with us?"

"Just overnight," I replied.

Oh, how wonderful that hot shower felt! It was great to get into clean clothes and lie out on that warm, soft bed! I turned on the TV and simply marveled at how big the world was. After some complimentary coffee and muffins from the front lobby, I loaded up my dirty clothes and headed to the laundromat.

It's incredible to me how one can grow accustomed to one's own smells in the woods, but once in civilization, at the mercy of soap and water, one realizes fairly quickly that one...well...stinks.

Picking up some laundry soap at the grocery store, I spent the rest of the morning washing and drying clothes. I had lunch at the Chocolate Moose and later felt guilty when the sun came out with all of its brilliance, and I chose to stay in town. I simply wanted to put yesterday's calamity out of my mind and seize the day. I went back to the hotel room and lay down for a wonderful nap. When I awoke it was sprinkling outside again, and the sun was nowhere in sight.

When early evening rolled around, I took a deep breath and called home, knowing Barb would be home from work.

"You're where?" she asked.

"A hotel in Ely," I replied.

"OK, so let me get this straight. You broke camp and went into Ely for the night? So, you'll be starting home tomorrow?"

"No, I didn't break camp. I just packed up my clothes and food and headed into town for a break from the crappy weather."

"So then, what you're telling me is that you're taking a break from your spiritual retreat?"

"Well, yeah, I guess. Sort of. Anyway, I'm going back to my campsite tomorrow and will be here a couple of more days. Then I'll be heading home."

"Well, OK then," she said hesitantly. "Nanc, you're sure everything's OK up there?"

"It's all OK. I'm just learning a whole lot and some of it's hard. I don't know how to process it, let alone explain it to you."

How could I tell her about the seventeen little memorial services? How could I explain about my spiritual life being a false bottom or the dancing loon line? How would I explain that I was journaling to God and a *voice* seemed to be giving me responses? What would she think if she knew I'd almost sunk the boat in forty feet of water? Or that I'd been cut by a boat propeller? How could I explain about the great revelation I'd had about trust?

She'd have thought I'd gone off the deep end, and then I'd have had to explain my irrational fear of deep things and my desire to dance on the water.... and it would only make matters worse.

"Barb," I said instead, "I'm really having a spiritual awakening. I love you, and I'll be starting for home by the end of the week. I came into town to get my clothes washed and to get dried out for a day or two. I'll head back to camp first thing in the morning. Now don't worry."

I know that it probably sounds strange, but in this tiny town of Ely, Minnesota, they actually have an old movie theatre. It's ancient, but the movie was a new release and the concession stand was affordable. I had a moment of guilt as I paid my admission and walked in the doors, but that was short-lived when an hour into the movie the projector turned off and the theatre manager came in to report that a tornado had touched down near Virginia and another one near Eveleth.

The bad weather appeared to be heading our way. The manager offered everyone's money back if we wanted to leave. I thought about it as I watched three or four people head for the door. Hmmm, the newer hotel or this old monstrous theatre? It didn't seem like much of a choice to me.

I bought another soda and watched the rest of the movie. I had a moment's thought about my campsite and boat but quickly realized that a tornado was well out of my control. I'd just have to wait and see what happened.

Leaving that night around 9:30 I was amazed at how ugly the sky had become. I drove quickly back to the hotel and felt much gratitude that I wasn't out in the woods. It had rained off and on, all day, and the last thing I wanted was to try to weather a tornado in a tent. I fell into a deep and restful sleep.

SPIRITUAL GROWTH: A PROCESS, NOT AN EVENT

The worst of the weather passed us by and in the morning, I drank coffee at the Moose as the fickle sun rose once again in the sky, leaving hues of pink, orange and blue. Folks at the table next to me were preparing to take a trip into the boundary waters, anxiously gathering weather reports from anyone who would talk with them. The consensus was that the next four to five days would be sunny and clear.

I could only smile. Yeah. Right.

I didn't head back to my campsite as early as I had planned. In fact, it was midafternoon before I left town. In one way I felt like a traitor. After all, I'd bailed out on my spiritual retreat, hadn't I? On the other hand, I had taken good care of myself. I had recognized my limitations and made a choice that seemed healthy for me.

Could this tie into what I had been learning on my spiritual retreat? If so, I hadn't bailed out on anything. Instead, I'd put some healthy personal priorities into place. It occurred to me that I felt way too much guilt in my life.

· · ·

I spent the rest of the afternoon drying out the campsite. Everything was damp but nothing a couple of hours on the clothesline, strung between trees, wouldn't fix. I'd picked up some dry wood up at the ranger station and, seeing a broom there beside the wood, I'd taken the opportunity to sweep up a bag of bark and scrap that had broken off the wood bundles. What I ended up with was a nice bag full of dry kindling. Next, I headed to the lake and spent a half-hour bailing the boat, again.

As I lit the fire to begin supper, Old One Match prevailed again. It was a great fire even though the coal bed was wet. It occurred to me that using dry wood with a wet coal bed could work. Had I not picked up those bundles of wood, I wouldn't have stood a chance of getting that fire going. Somehow, I was feeling better. I realized that over the past week and a half I'd gained a better feeling about life in general. When things looked their worst, there were still choices to be made and possibilities to be had. It had been several days since I'd had the *"I'm so tired"* thought come into my mind. In fact, I was feeling refreshed and excited about the next couple of days. I knew they would be my last days there as it was time to think about going home.

I missed my family a lot, but I couldn't say that I missed the church responsibilities and never-ending work. I had enjoyed being far away where I wasn't "on-call" twenty-four hours a day, seven days a week. Although I'd wondered about the worship services I'd missed, I truly wasn't concerned. One of the most capable members had been left in charge of those services and the preaching. I just wasn't quite ready to return to it all yet.

I was relieved when the answering machine picked up on the day I went to the ranger station to call the church. I knew I was supposed to call a designated church leader if I was going to stay any of the extra time they had allotted me, so I was faithful in making that call to give them plenty of time to plan for my absence.

Little did I know that some of the church leaders had been doing some planning of their own in my absence.

I would later learn that those plans were for the future of the church, and they didn't include me.

. . .

That evening was a perfect Ely evening. The sunset was brilliant in its oranges and reds. I took what promised to be a great shot of two loons swimming across the lake in the sunset. The walleyes were biting, and I enjoyed catching and releasing them one after the other. I knew that once the sky darkened to blues and grays, I would need to start back across the lake but sitting there with the gentle waves lapping against the shore, smelling the depths of the forest, and listening to the symphony of the woods beginning to play out, I felt as if I were in heaven.

A short time later as I went across the lake, the motor humming, I saw the trees of the small islands silhouetted against the water. It was beautiful, simply beautiful. I felt tears well in my eyes as I shouted loud above the motor, "Thank You, God! I love you!" My image of God had certainly grown!

That night as the fire danced merrily in the fire pit, I looked up to see the stars shining brightly in the sky. I didn't know what the next day would bring, but I knew that in the presence of the moment I had peace in my heart. As I breathed in the smells of the woods it was as though I were breathing in God. I cannot say the last time I had felt so at peace and fulfilled in the world.

It was almost midnight before I climbed into my sleeping bag and fell into a deep sleep. Yes, things were definitely shifting within me. A huge part of what I was learning was that spiritual growth is a process, not an event.

Journal Entry:

Good morning, God! What a glorious morning it is! As I sit here drinking my coffee I take in the marvelous smells of the forest. No incense of any church has ever smelled more holy. I watch as the chipmunks, the squirrels and the birds take communion with me this morning. Bread and cookies serve as the elements, and together we fellowship. The birds in the trees are singing a closing hymn. My writing in this journal is the benediction. May you bless this day and everything in it. No matter what

the day might bring, may I find you in the midst of every situation.
Amen.

THE PRESENCE OF THE MOMENT

This was my second to the last full day here in the woods. Two more nights in my sleeping bag, and it would be time to break camp. I could barely believe that I had been there for almost two weeks. I watched the bacon cooking in the cast iron skillet and poured another cup of coffee. This was the good life. My goal for the day was to stay, as I had been practicing, in the present moment and to look for the Sacred in everything.

After breakfast, I washed the dishes and put everything away. I then began to gather kindling for the supper's fire. The blue skies fueled my optimism, but I remained cautious. I split some logs and then tucked everything under the tarp so that it would stay dry if the rains came. I zipped up the windows and door to the tent and made sure I had water, munchies and camera equipment. I knew, odd is it may sound after my rage, that God would provide me with the rest.

I drove up to the ranger station to let them know I was hiking Blueberry Lake on this fine day, and that I planned to be back at the station by 4:00 pm. If I was not back by 6:00 pm I knew they would send someone looking for me. We agreed on the times and I drove up toward the Primitive Campground. I knew that the path leading back to and around Blueberry Lake was found up in this area.

Parking the Jeep, I grabbed my backpack with the water and munchies and slung my camera across my shoulders. This would be, approximately, a four-mile hike through the deeper part of the woods where the trail is often nothing more than a deer path. I was very excited to begin this venture. The park rangers had told me that if I wanted to see moose and bears in the woods, this would be the place I'd likely see them. I planned to move quietly so as to not scare away the deer, but I was prepared to make a lot of noise if I saw a bear or moose! I would, of course, snap a few shots first.

The trail was overgrown with thick tangles of brush. I was barely into the hike when a great stick seemed to present itself. It was an ideal hiking stick and I gratefully accepted the gift nature offered. Moving through the woods I stumbled here and there, on ankle-twisting obstacles. The hiking stick proved to be a godsend.

The sun in the sky shared that it was around noon when I stopped for lunch. The menu was nothing more elaborate than water, trail mix and some fruit, but I found it refreshing. Pulling out my camera I took some macro-zoom shots of various flora and fauna in the area.

About an hour later, I made it to Blueberry Lake and stopped to rest. I chose a grassy place within a foot of the lake, startling a buck from behind a nearby pine. I was so busy watching this magnificent creature staring back at me, I didn't get a picture. After a minute or two, he meandered off into a thicket, evidently deciding that I posed no risk. It was absolutely tranquil. The lake was like glass. I sat listening to complete silence broken only by the occasional cry of a distant loon.

My knee was aching again. I dug out some Tylenol from my pocket and swallowed them with water from the canteen. While digging deep for the small tablets, my fingers wrapped around the medicine bag. I brought it out noting that it was beginning to look used. There were dirt smudges on the light leather and a couple of the colorful beads were coming loose. While this sort of wear and tear on traditional religious articles would have bothered me, I liked the idea that this bag was to be used rather than displayed on someone's altar.

I lay back on the soft grass watching the cloud shapes drift slowly overhead. The next thing I knew I woke up. The sun hadn't moved very far so I guessed I'd napped for about an hour.

My knee felt better, and I stood up with a last look around before resuming my hike around the lake. The park ranger had warned me that I'd lose the trail as I continued around the lake. She directed me to just keep following the lake, watching for the trail to pick up again on the other side.

I came to a rocky part of the path, deeper into the thick of the trees. It was darker here, and a thick and heavy bedding of pine needles covered the ground. I stepped over rock after rock as I carefully picked my way through this area.

Suddenly, looking down at the rocks ahead, I saw garter snakes. Lots of them! They were squirming and slithering all around the place. Part of me felt repulsed, as the snake is not one of my favorite creatures. But still, I seemed to have disturbed something sacred. Not wanting to step on them, and not wishing to trip and fall, I picked my way along carefully. I'd always thought snakes were nasty creatures. Walking through them, it occurred to me that this was their habitat, and I was an interloper.

Stepping gingerly, I chuckled to myself as I said, "Sorry, excuse me, sorry."

Glad to be past the rocks and snakes I hiked around the other side of the lake and watched for the path to pick up again. I stopped to sit and rest. As I sat there, I was privileged to hear a symphony of sorts: The *Concerto of the Northern Leopard Frogs* was in full swing. I gave up trying to figure out where the sounds were coming from; I was content to just sit back and listen.

I drove up to the ranger station at about 4:15 that afternoon. I bought some more ice and asked about something I'd found on my way back up the main trail. I had paused to shoot what I thought was a fungus of some sort, but soon realized it wasn't a plant at all. Picking it up and smelling it, I realized it was something relating to an animal! Looking more closely I saw a large pile of bones including a skull. As I described it to one of the rangers, I saw a look of astonishment on his face.

He said, "Wow. What you're describing is a wolf kill. That's the way the wolf pack leaves the deer after they've eaten all the meat they want. They leave a bunch of bones and a pile of fur. You found something the average camper doesn't find, lady."

I was speechless.

When I returned to the campsite, legs tired and stomach growling, I started the fire and kicked back in my chair to ponder the day. I was anxious to see the results of the seven rolls of film I'd already taken: trees, birds, chipmunks, squirrels, loons, deer, fungi, stumps, flowers, and of course the lake. I think I actually dozed in the chair for a few minutes as the pine logs snapped and popped in the energetic fire.

Relaxation seemed so foreign to me before I arrived at Bear Head. Now I was light of heart, mind, spirit and emotions. This trip was a gift I'd given myself, and God had surely blessed it.

After supper, while watching the coals burn down and die out, I sat and wrote in my journal.

Dear God,

I know I have neglected you this past year and a half. I know that I have blamed you for the bad things that have happened to me and accused you of abandoning me. I haven't had my priorities in order, to say the least. In fact, there have been times when you were the least of my priorities. I am so sorry. I hope that in your mercy and grace there will be forgiveness for me. I've felt like such a wounded warrior. How could I truly believe that I was strong enough to survive all that I have been through without help? What I know today is this: You are the Creator. You are the one who created me; You knew me as I was being knit together in my mother's womb. You know the number of hairs on my head. I know that you called me to be a pastor. I know that you called me to resign from my former church and move my family to our new home and town. I know that you called me to this church. I truly don't understand everything that's been happening along the way, but I believe that you are holding me in the palm of your gentle hand. Thank you for the moment I first knew that I needed help. Thank you for reminding me about Ely and my past trips here. Thank you for Bear Head Lake State Park and for the miracle you are working in my heart while I am here. For I know now, in this very moment, that I will return to my church a new creature. I know that I am not called to resign my credentials, and I believe that you will give me the strength and insight to pastor the church you have placed in my care. I love you, and I am very grateful. And just as you've taught me about the importance of priorities in camping, (I won't forget about waterproofing the tent next time) help me to learn about healthy priorities in my daily living.

ANGEL IN THE WOODS

I took the boat out a little early, hoping to go for a spin around the one bay I hadn't yet explored. This bay was on the other side of the point, so I was hoping to be in my fishing spot right on time. Of course, I hadn't worn a watch in over a week, so I never knew if I was a little late or a little early because time no longer mattered.

I was puttering around the bend when, right overhead, flew a bald eagle! I watched as it flew majestically over the lake and the trees, landing on a huge dead tree overlooking the water. I brought the boat around, and while the waves tossed it to and fro, I managed to put on the six-hundred mirror lens and get off a couple of shots. My hope was that, in spite of the rocking of the boat, and having no tripod, I would still get a clean shot. Obviously, I believed in miracles!

While I sat at the point fishing, the eagle sat perched in that dead tree. When darkness began to descend upon the now tranquil and quiet lake, the eagle flew off to places unknown.

As I brought in my line and took the last leech of the night off the hook, I heard the howling begin. And as the wolves howled into the night sky, I heard another, higher pitched howl, almost a scream. I can honestly tell you that I had never before heard such a sound.

I thought about the wolf kill I had discovered earlier in the day and wondered about the sorts of things that happened at Blueberry Lake after dark. I became aware of the hair standing straight up on the back of my neck and my arms. I felt a sudden chill and was quite ready to get back to the warmth and light of a campfire.

As I pulled hard, the motor roared to life, and I reached down and brought up the anchor. The howling continued over the din of the motor, and I beat a hasty retreat out across the water. It was still and quiet once again while I carefully docked and tied up the boat. With one last glance back at the fading light, I hiked up over the steep, rugged incline and took the path leading to my campsite.

Today is my last full day here. I am saddened to be leaving, but ready to see Barb & Zachary. I hope to go into the east bay today and spot some loons. I'd love to get a good loon shot before leaving tomorrow. I hope it doesn't rain because packing up everything wet will be a pain; but I will accept life as it comes, knowing that I will receive the strength I need.

This was my journal entry as I sat by the morning fire drinking my third cup of coffee. Soon I would clean up and do the dishes before heading out to the lake.

First, however, I found myself opening the medicine bag. Such an assortment of things in this little bag! I put aside the things that the Indian women had placed in it. Then smiling, I looked at the special things I had added to the bag. Each one carried with it a memory of something sacred I had experienced there in the woods. I chuckled as I thought about how I would explain these items to another person. Then it occurred to me that I didn't have to explain them to anyone. This was my medicine, personal and private. I had been trained, since adolescence, to share my faith beliefs with everyone. This was totally different. It wasn't that I felt ashamed or embarrassed. No, these artifacts were completely ME and completely SACRED. I paused again for a moment of gratitude before adding the original items, recognizing that they represented love.

. . .

Snap. Snap. I got off a couple of shots as I used the trolling motor to get around the back bay. I discovered a loon nestled up against the bank of one of the islands. The loon was drinking water and I hoped I captured some of it on film. I was careful to respect the loon's space, along with the two adult loons and their precious brown baby, I spotted shortly thereafter. Using larger lenses made this respect possible. Of course, how these shots would turn out from the rocking boat was questionable.

It amazed me to watch as these gorgeous creatures swam along together so elegantly in the water. This little family of three made me homesick for my own family, and I was reminded that this time tomorrow I'd be in the car heading for home.

Sitting out there on the water I found myself thinking about my church. I knew that it was not the end of the road for me as a pastor, but I still felt concerned about how effective I would be when I got home. After all, I still had a great deal of grief and loss work to do. My time in the woods had been just the beginning. This scripture passage from Proverbs came to me:

In all thy ways acknowledge God and God will direct your paths.

A clear message. If I trusted God for the direction and the plan, God would provide. Despite the grief and loss work that still lay ahead of me, I was going to be just fine. That acknowledgment gave me strength.

I went back to the campsite and took some time to write in my journal. As I sat there writing and recalling the experiences I'd had in the past two weeks, I was reminded of being a child in grade school writing about what I did on my summer vacation. With a smile on my face, I used that concept to write the following:

Things I Learned on My Spiritual Retreat

- *You can pray as hard as you can, but it still might rain.*

- *Careful and timely priorities with careful preparation can prevent disaster.*
- *Never, Never, Never assume the tent is still water-proofed.*
- *If you kick the boat plug out in forty feet of water, don't sit and bail, and never underestimate the potential of a stick of butter.*
- *Always be sure both motors are off, especially when you're in the water.*
- *Change can be difficult, but not the end of the world. In fact, change offers a new beginning.*
- *You cannot deal successfully with situations by ignoring them.*
- *The sun can still shine amidst the rain; don't miss out on the rainbow!*
- *Stop worrying about what other people think. It doesn't matter!*
- *When your bladder wakes you up at 2:00 in the morning, look for the blessing.*
- *Bad things are simply challenges to help us grow.*
- *Take time for personal spirituality every day; make it life's #1 priority.*
- *Plan an annual spiritual retreat alone, in a place that inspires.*
- *Life flows like a river. Go with the flow.*
- *Not all things are what they appear to be; watch out for false bottoms.*

As I lit the fire for the last supper of the trip, I smiled as Old One Match did her thing. I wondered how I'd adjust to plain old food once I left the fire scar behind. I made the decision to wash things up and began to pack the cooking trunk. In the morning I would stop for breakfast as I traveled back toward the Twin Cities. I knew that I could stay until 4:00 o'clock check-out time, but now, resolved to leave, I wanted to be on the road the first thing in the morning.

A little later, I had the distinct feeling that I was to load the boat that evening rather than wait until morning. Call it God speaking to me, intuition, heightened awareness, or all three. I stopped and reflected on the feeling. I didn't want to miss another evening's fishing. But I got the feeling again. It was clear that I needed to go ahead and get the boat ready. I feel strangely at peace about this. When had I learned to trust that still voice within me?

I drove the Jeep over to the boat ramp. Then I walked back around the small bay using the beach trail to get the boat. I took it out for one last run across the lake, then brought it back and tied it up by the boat ramp.

While I'd been a nervous wreck about unloading the boat properly, I didn't feel nervous at all about what others might think as I backed the Jeep and trailer down the ramp. Of course, I hadn't seen anyone, besides the rangers, for days.

I brought the boat up and onto the trailer with relative ease. Pulling out of the lake, and up and around the bend, however, I realized that the boat was not on the trailer as straight as it should be. I parked the Jeep and went back to see if I was strong enough to muscle it. I wasn't. I quickly saw the need to take the seventy-five-pound motor off, then position the boat correctly. I would then have to lift the motor back up onto the boat again.

Feeling calm and secure about what I needed to do, I moved to unlock the motor from the steel bar that held it securely on the boat. I looked up to see a man in jeans and a white t-shirt coming through the woods. He was not on a path, and I thought that seemed rather strange. He was simply coming through the thicket.

He smiled at me with warm eyes and said, "Hello. I've come to help." I felt goose bumps all over me. "Here, I've got it," he said as he lifted the boat and motor and positioned them squarely on the trailer. He said nothing more. He just turned, smiling, heading back into the woods.

I called out, "Thank you very much!" He turned back slightly, still smiling, and waved as he continued walking to wherever he was heading.

I've had a lot of thoughts since that day. Where did he come from? How did he know what I needed? Why didn't he chat, like the park rangers, and other people I'd met in the woods? Who was he? And the inevitable question: was he some sort of angel? I have no answers. What I do know is that God met my need in that moment. I finished tying down the boat, then took the few remaining leeches down to the lake to let them go. I stood by the water watching them swim off. Before I had time to think I was saying out loud:

God, I thank you for these blessed waters. Thank you for the fish I caught and for those I didn't. Bless these waters that they may continue to be a blessing to all your creation. Bless these leeches that they may be all you created them to be. Amen.

Good grief! I'd just blessed a lake, some fish and half a dozen leeches out loud in front of God and anyone else who might have been within earshot. And all I could do was grin.

That night I sat around the campfire and felt my heart singing. I was so grateful for that fire, for the campsite, for the trees, foliage and the creatures of the woods. When I arrived I could only see the groomed trails. Now I was tuned into the flowers, the moss and ferns, the birds and all of God's creation. I was grateful for the sounds of the loons off in the distance and for the experiences, I had had out on the lake. My skin was browner, and my muscles were stronger. My self-confidence had risen beyond measure. My thoughts were positive and my prayers very personal and intimate. I clutched the medicine bag close to me and wondered when exactly I'd first embraced it.

I turned in by 10:00 that night, leaving the front flap of the tent open so that I could lie there and see the stars through the screen mesh. I knew that it would be chillier like this and that at some point during the night I would likely get up and zip up the flap, but I would deal with that when and if I needed to. I no longer saw it as an inconvenience but as an opportunity. For now, I was simply enjoying the presence of the moment. I slept peacefully through the night.

The next morning as I sat having my last cup of coffee, I watched the coals die out. Everything was packed neatly into the Jeep except for my journal and pen, my coffee cup, and me.

I wrote my final journal entry:

My life has become a prayer. God is in everything.... a raindrop on a leaf, the stars so huge and low. The haunting cry of the loon while I lie in my tent now brings me comfort. The soaring scream of the eagle flying over my campsite on this last morning brings me joy. Sitting with the sunset...feeling the tug of yet another walleye makes me laugh out loud.

I now notice that God is in everything, and I am in God. The wind rustles the leaves and I listen so as to hear God's voice and to know and experience the breath of God even if just for the moment.

My hair is lighter. My skin is darker. My body is stronger. My life has new confidence, meaning and purpose. I am needed – by me.

As I pack on this final morning, I feel a deep renewal of my "self". I also feel a sadness at leaving this all behind.

And when did I stop being so afraid of all deep things? (smiling)

I reflect on my hike to Blueberry Lake. I think about the wolf kill and the bear that ran across the road in front of me; I picture the deer that ran across my path stopping to lock eyes with me for only a moment. What an intimate moment. And then my mind drifts to the two loons with their tiny brown baby, and the loon line dance I'd been privileged to watch that special night. I think about the chips and squirrels and wiggly garter snakes; the majestic eagle, the night of the celestial lights...and the sacred gift who came through the woods to help me with the boat last night.

As I sit here, I breathe in the woods. I breathe in God.

Soon I'll be driving back down I-35 South. The fuel gauge on the Jeep reads full. The gauge on my spiritual life also reads full. It's time, but I still have a reluctance to go. It's not that I don't miss my family. It's just a sense of deep loss I am feeling as I prepare to leave. I'm not ready for the noisy world with all of its sensory stimulation. I'm not ready for the "So did you have a good time?" and "Did you take any pictures?" There are no adequate words to describe what I have touched and what has touched me. The photographs may turn out great, but they can never capture the sheer magnificence of God I found in these woods.

As I drink my coffee, I think about my "goodbye" with the lake last night. It has been such a privilege to fish her waters and silently reverence her sunsets.

I now look around my campsite. For the fire, the space itself, the rocks and trees and creatures who shared so generously with me, I am grateful.

As I closed the journal and climbed into the Jeep, I found myself saying out loud, "So long, Bear Head Lake. See you next time."

And as I turned onto Hwy 169 thirty minutes later, I realized that I was out of the woods. At least for now.

OUT OF THE WOODS

I wish I could tell you that I returned home and lived happily ever after. My process through the grief and loss, however, was only beginning. I was physically out of the woods, but the internal journey was really just starting.

"Oh, Mama! I missed you so much!" Zach rushed at me as I climbed out of the Jeep. "I love you, Mama. Did God find you in the woods?"

"Oh Baby, I missed you too! I thought about you every day. And yes, God found me. We had a wonderful time together."

"Out of the mouths of babes," I laughed later that night. "What exactly did you tell him about my trip?"

"After you left," Barb replied, "he wanted to know why you needed to go to the woods to rest. I told him you were searching for a special quiet time with God. He asked me if God could find you way up in the north woods, and I assured him that God can find us no matter where we go."

"Interesting," I said reflectively. "Rather than me going to find God, he worried about God finding me."

"It sounds like you and God had a special connection up there. Did God come back with you?" She grinned.

"God was always with me," I said quietly, "I just needed to take God out of the church and experience our Creator in a new light."

"Out of the church? I thought the church was God's home."

"Do you remember when we first met?" I asked. "You played on two softball teams, three volleyball teams, a basketball team, and you golfed. I saw you as a jock. Then, the day I brought you lunch at work, I saw you as a physical therapist and I was amazed at your skill. I've seen you in many different lights over the years: friend, lover, jock, mother, physical therapist, daughter and more."

"Yeah," she said quietly, trying to conceptualize it.

"I'd only ever seen God in church."

Her eyes lit up with recognition. "So, you learned new things about God because you saw God in a different context."

"Exactly!"

"That's pretty cool, honey. I want to hear more about it. Come talk to me while I put the steaks on the grill."

We walked outside into the delightful Oklahoma sunshine. While Barb watched the steaks, Zach and I lay down on the grass and tried to find shapes in the white billowy clouds overhead.

"So, what are your thoughts about the church?" Barb asked as she joined us there on our backs.

"I feel renewed and revived," I said. "I think it's all going to work out just fine."

"Look, Mama," Zach exclaimed in childish wonder, "I see a church in the clouds. Do you see it, Mama?"

I wasn't sure I did, but then as I followed his little finger with my eyes, I came across a shape that *did* resemble a traditional church, complete with a steeple.

"Speaking of the church," I began, "how have things been going there?"

"Okay," Barb replied, taking a deep breath. "Stephanie did a great job leading the service and preaching. I know you're not surprised about that. She has a wonderful spirit about her. Lots of people asked if we'd heard from you, and I told them that you seemed to be enjoying yourself. I did hear a snide remark from one of your Trustees. He mumbled something about it sounding an awful lot like a vacation rather than a retreat. It was all I could do to keep my mouth shut."

"Wow," I said with surprise. "The Trustees were supportive. I'm surprised he'd say such a thing."

"The other Trustees didn't speak to us," she continued, "with the exception of Kate. She asked if I'd heard from you but didn't look like she wanted the answer. It was awkward, to say the least."

"I'll bet," I replied slowly, puzzled at the behavior of these people.

"I didn't know if I should tell you that or not," she said, "but we don't keep secrets from each other."

"I'm glad you told me," I said reluctantly. I felt that old knot in my stomach begin to tie up again.

MUTINY

Our church service began at 11:00 on Sunday mornings. Our worship team had the responsibility for setting up for the service between 10:00 and 10:30. I usually arrived by 10:15. On my first Sunday back, I felt an excitement I hadn't felt in a long time. I'd prepared a sermon I was jazzed about. So jazzed I didn't even need notes! It was committed to memory, and I'd gone over it time and time again as I wanted the delivery to be dynamic. I hadn't felt that way about a sermon since we'd first arrived in Evanston. They were going to see that time away had been beneficial and I was ready to embrace ministry with them!

I left home at 9:15, too excited to wait.

"Zach and I aren't going that early," Barb said. "That's too long to keep him occupied. We'll drive separately and see you there."

We shared a kiss as Zach wrapped his arms around our legs and cried out, "My moms are mooching!" We all three laughed as I went out the door.

I turned on the lights in the sanctuary. Everything was exactly as I had left it. I checked in my office for notes and phone messages and was surprised to see none. I started the coffee, then walked up behind the pulpit. Rubbing my hands across its smooth wood finish I wondered what my life would have held if I'd come back to resign. Aloud I said, "Thank you for renewing and reviving me, God. I'm ready to serve you through this congregation."

At 10:00 I peeked outside to see who was arriving to set up for the service. My Jeep was the only vehicle in the parking lot. I walked back to my office and sat down to pray for the service.

I looked at my watch and saw that it was 10:15. Funny, I hadn't heard anyone out in the sanctuary. I walked out and saw that it was as empty as it had been before. Thinking that perhaps I hadn't thoroughly unlocked the doors, I went to check. The worship team had their own keys, but maybe the person on the schedule for the morning had forgotten their key. The door was unlocked.

Peeking out at the parking lot again, I saw that the Jeep was still alone. An uneasy feeling crept across me. People would begin to arrive between 10:30 and 10:45. There were no bulletins, the altar was not set up for communion, and the music for that week was nowhere in sight. I didn't want to take over other people's tasks, but the waiting was laborious. What was going on?

At 10:40 I set up the altar for communion. At 10:45, the first parishioners began to arrive. I was greeted warmly by Stephanie and her partner, Sherrie. They shared in my surprise that no one had come to set up for worship. I thought I saw an unsettled look in Stephanie's eyes. As others arrived, I welcomed them, noting out of the corner of my eye that the bulletins had, at some point, arrived and the announcements were set out. The full board of trustees was present, but none of them made eye contact with me.

I changed into my vestments with Stephanie's assistance.

"I heard you preached a couple of excellent sermons," I told her as she straightened my chasuble.

"Well," she replied, "you're a pretty hard act to follow." We both laughed.

I said, "Maybe after this week. I really had a wonderful experience of renewal and revival, Stephanie."

"I'm glad, Pastor," she said quietly. "I think you're going to need it."

Before I could question her, she said quickly, "Okay, it's time. Have a great service."

Standing before my congregation was, as always, a humbling experience. Delightful faces looked at me expectantly. It was the first time they had seen me without the eye patch since I'd lost vision in my right eye. I began by saying that it was wonderful to be back. I continued to say that my eyesight remained stable and I was grateful beyond words. I thanked Stephanie for sharing her worship gifts with the church in my absence, then thanked the Board of Trustees for allowing me to take this time for a spiritual retreat. Not one of them looked at me. Their heads were either down or looking in another direction.

Something was definitely wrong. Despite the dis-ease in the pit of my stomach, I preached from my gut. After the service, over coffee, many people came to tell me how happy they were to have me back. Not one trustee spoke to me or acknowledged me. In fact, they were quickly out the door after counting the offering.

"I have a bad feeling about this," I said to Barb over Sunday dinner. Zach was happily playing in his mash potatoes as we talked, oblivious to anything but hiding his peas under the blanket of gravy.

"It doesn't sound good to me," Barb replied. "I just don't understand them. They give you the time away, then act as if you've done something wrong. Talk about passive-aggressive!"

"I don't know what to think, but I'm going to spend some time in prayer this afternoon."

"Sounds like a plan," she said. "When Zach goes down for his nap, I'll join you."

I was in my office bright and early the next morning when the phone rang. It was Kate. Kate was a quiet trustee who appeared to be silently supportive of me. At least I never had heard anything negative from her. I often thought that it must be difficult for her to be a trustee. The others were her good friends, yet she obviously didn't act like them. I wasn't sure what she believed but hoped she was with me. I quickly learned that she was, indeed, with me as I listened to her on the other end of the line.

"Pastor, this is really hard for me. I don't want anyone to get mad at me, but there's something you need to know. While you were gone the board tried to hold a meeting to figure out how to fire you."

"What!" I cried. "Fire me for what?"

"For going away for those weeks. And there's still concern you will lose your eyesight completely and won't be able to fully pastor this church."

"But the Board of Trustees *gave* me that time away. They told me to take longer if I needed. And, I announced in church that my vision appeared to be stabilized."

"I know," she said sadly. "I reminded them that they told you to take three weeks away if you needed it. I showed them the bylaws. According to Article IV viii. 3. the Board of Trustees cannot meet in such a capacity without the pastor's knowledge. Boy, are they mad at me!"

"I'm surprised they didn't meet anyway," I said as my stomach rolled over.

"They may have," she said. "I told them that I would have no part of it. I just wanted to give you a heads up. I'm so sorry about this. You don't deserve it. I am glad your eye is doing so well. At least that's one good thing!"

"I came back refreshed and revived, ready to take on ministry with all of its joys and challenges," I said, my voice choking with emotion. "I don't know what to do now."

"Pastor," she began softly, "if I were you, I'd contact the bishop for some help. I honestly think you're going to need it."

"The bishop?" I said with surprise. "You think this is that serious?"

"Don't kid yourself," she said slowly. "These people play hardball. This is far from over."

As I placed the phone back on its cradle, I lowered my head to my hands and wept.

. . .

Contacting the trustees to tell them about the bishop's upcoming visit, seemed to throw fuel on the fire. They wouldn't respond to my phone calls. If they attended worship services in the coming weeks, they slipped in after it started and slipped out before the benediction. There was no way I could deal directly with them. The bishop recommended I send them a letter stating that since there was obviously a problem, and they were unable to meet with me to resolve it, the bishop would be coming to mediate and foster reconciliation. A date was set and, although I was nervous, I believed that this was the best course of action. I wanted to fight for my pastorate, fight for my church!

ANIMAL SPIRITS

Two Sundays after my return home from the woods, my Native American friends approached me after the worship service.

"Tell us about the four-legged and winged ones you encountered," asked Margaret Raven Feather, a gleam in her eye.

"Well, I saw deer, squirrels, loons, eagles, chipmunks, a beaver and a bear," I recited from memory. I could visualize each one as I said its name, and I knew a smile was radiating over my face at each memory.

"My, my, my," was the response from Margaret.

"This IS exciting," exclaimed Allison Snow Owl.

"What do you mean?" I asked puzzled.

"Well," began Allison, "the deer can remind you that there are times to stay and times to run away."

"Wow!" I responded. "How do you know that?"

"And the squirrels remind you to store up what you have for another day. They remind us to make sure we're prepared for the future," continued Margaret.

"When eagle comes into our lives, we know that whatever process is happening in our lives, will begin to speed up and move much more quickly than we expect," chimed in Allison. "And the loon takes you deeper into your greatest hopes and dreams. It tells us that we shouldn't compromise the opportunities in our lives; we need to stand up and go for it!"

"But how do you know all this?" I pleaded.

"Whew, we have our work cut out for us," laughed Margaret.

"And the bear asks you to question yourself."

"About what?" I asked them.

"About whether you're being realistic about situations in your life," Margaret replied. "When Bear comes into your life you need to ask yourself if you are being realistic or looking at life through rose-colored glasses."

"And the beaver is important as well," said Allison. "The beaver reminds us of the importance of home and family. It's important to take good care of our loved ones, to protect them and the family home above all others."

"Oh," I said with utter confusion. "These animals really do mean something then?"

They sat there smiling through my discomfort.

"Did any others come to you?" asked Margaret.

"Well, I saw a wolf kill, and heard wolf howls several nights."

"My, my, my," giggled Margaret, her eyes sparkling.

"This is powerful, sister," replied Allison. "Wolf is a teacher and a guardian. When Wolf comes into your life, you're going to take a new path. Wolf will help protect you as you make the change and will also help teach you the things you will need to know."

"What else?" asked Margaret with a twinkle in her eye.

"Snakes," I said, hesitantly. "Lots of garter snakes."

"Oh my gosh," gushed Allison. "The snake represents transmutation. When it sheds its skin, it becomes brand new. It reminds us that we too have to shed our old skins and enter into a newness of life."

"But how do you know all this?" I asked again.

Margaret ignored my question.

"Did you have any experiences with the bag we gave you?"

I told them about the things I'd added to my medicine bag and about the feather disappearing. They smiled. I asked about some of the items they had placed in the bag. I soon learned that the contents included sage, a turtle claw, a coyote claw, earth, a wolf tooth, and sweet grass. I was amazed!

"Can you explain all this to me?" I asked.

"Absolutely," they replied, almost in unison.

"This is why we've been called to your life, Pastor. How about coffee tomorrow afternoon, at the Coffee Clutch, around 1:00?" asked Allison.

"Okay," I replied. "I'll be there. Should I bring anything?"

"Just bring the wolf," said Margaret. I could hear their guffaws as they walked out the door.

Bring the wolf? What in the world had I gotten myself into?

THIRTY DAYS

The bishop and I met for lunch a few hours prior to our meeting with the board of trustees. I had no relationship with him other than brief encounters at various church conferences.

"I'm certainly hoping we can do some good work tonight, Bishop," I said as I buttered a roll. "I think there's some real potential in this congregation. Now that I am on my feet and working through the grief and loss issues with a therapist, I'm ready to give this church the best I have to give."

"I hope so too," he replied as he cut into his roast beef. "There is no reason why we can't work through these issues and put them behind us."

That evening we gathered in the meeting room of the church. The entire board of trustees was present. Kate was the only one who looked at me. She caught my eye momentarily, then looked away, her face red. Her discomfort was evident. I noted that Lou had her Bible with her. There were yellow sticky notes throughout. I found myself wondering what part of the scripture she planned to use against me. I felt profound sadness at seeing the Word of God used as a weapon.

The bishop led us in prayer and then asked the board of trustees if any of them would like to begin the conversation. There was silence.

"I am willing to share my perspective," I began after a long pregnant pause.

"No, I want to hear from the board," replied the bishop with a chastising tone in his voice.

Again, there was no response.

Finally, the bishop stated emphatically, "If no one is willing to work through this situation there can be no reconciliation. Without reconciliation this church cannot continue to function effectively."

"Well," I said cautiously, "I am willing to work through this situation."

Incredibly, the bishop looked daggers at me. "If I want to hear from you, I will ask for it."

I sat there stunned as the board of trustees looked at one another with little grins of satisfaction. Only Kate sat with her head down, not looking at anyone.

Another five minutes went by in this bizarre meeting. I watched Lou flip through her Bible, and I was tempted to bait her. I didn't want to risk the bishop's bite, however, so I kept quiet.

"Does anyone have anything to say?" asked the bishop impatiently, casting a warning glance my way.

It occurred to me that I was being set up. If the board of trustees refused to work on reconciliation, the church couldn't function in a healthy manner. Without reconciliation, I couldn't stay there and pastor with good conscience. I was not going to allow the bishop the opportunity to ask for my resignation. As I came to this realization, I began to grow angry. It wasn't my fault that the house fell through, or my brother died. It wasn't my fault that my dog died or any of those people died within such a short span of time. It wasn't my fault that I lost the sight in my eye. I was tired of not having control in my life while still being blamed for not functioning at their expected level of professionalism.

Saying a silent prayer to the God of the woods I felt my spirit quiet. I pictured the deer, the squirrel, the loons, the eagles, the bear and the wolf-kill in my mind. They flashed before me as I heard these words and ideas: teacher, guide, knowing when to stay and when to go, transmutation, change is coming quickly, be careful of looking at the world through rose-colored glasses, prepare for the future, go deeper with your hopes and dreams rather than settling for less.

The words, and their meaning, flashed through my mind. As tears of relief and peace sprang to my eyes, I heard these words come out of my mouth, "Please accept my resignation as your pastor. This is my official thirty-day notice."

You could have heard a pin drop for the next ten seconds. Then the room exploded into a fury of angry voices.

"You have GOT to be kidding me!" screamed Mattie. "After all we've done for you and your family, you think you can just walk out on us?"

Before I could respond, Patrice yelled, "You're just using us. You've used us from the start!"

"Used you how?" I exclaimed in utter shock.

"You'll be an elder one day. You used us as a steppingstone to further your own self-serving goals. You waltzed in here and took advantage of us. Now you're waltzing back out. Well, good riddance, lady!"

Other board members began to speak their minds in the same tone. Lou paged through her Bible furiously. As she opened her mouth to quote scripture at me, I decided I'd had enough.

"I have a few things I'm going to say to you now," I began, my voice trembling.

"Oh no you don't," replied the bishop. "We're taking a twenty-minute break."

With that, the bishop and all of the board, except for one, got up and walked out the doors of the church. I sat there alone with Kate. She was sobbing into her hands. I sat there for a few minutes. Realizing that there was to be no conversation, I got up, moved to my office and picked up the phone.

"Nancy, what's going on over there?" Barb asked when she heard my trembling voice on the other end.

Holding back the tears I replied, "They ripped me a new asshole. It's bad, Barb. I resigned."

"Thank God," she replied. "Are you going to stay the thirty days?"

"I want to honor my contract. God will help me. I'd better get back out there. If it gets any uglier, I'm walking out and driving home."

"Promise?" Barb asked, her voice quaking.

"Promise," I responded.

The next hour was spent negotiating a severance package. It was hard to sit there listening to them argue about how much to give me. It was harder to hear them talk about the things I didn't deserve.

In the midst of it, one of the trustees stood up and said, "I've had enough of this shit. I'm out of here." With that, she walked out the door.

After another fifteen minutes of their bickering, I stood up and announced, "I will accept whatever you decide. I am honoring my contract with you by staying another thirty days. I believe you will honor it by making good decisions."

As I walked out the door, I heard Mattie say, "Oh screw you." Those words were directly aimed at me.

The bishop left the next morning. At least I presume he did because I didn't hear from him again. The board of trustees sent me a letter outlining, in detail, the severance package and their expectations of me during the next thirty days. They were clear, in the letter, that they were doing only what was required by the bishop. They were not interested in any of his recommendations. To this day, I'm not sure what he thought about this congregation and its pastor.

It was the longest thirty days of my life, but when I walked out the door for the last time it was with a strong sense of relief.

REFLECTIONS ON THE WOODS:

I continued to see the grief and loss counselor who had been so concerned for me before my trip to the woods and took some time over the next two months to travel, rest and write. As a result, I continued to experience the healing of my body, mind and spirit.

I was hired as a chaplain at a local Evanston nursing home. It was nice to have the income, but even nicer to work in a positive environment. During the coming months, I looked for the next church and met weekly with Allison and Margaret. I also used this time to write in the journal I'd started in the woods.

I came out of the woods ready to go! I was sure that I'd return to pastor this church to the best of my ability. I had no thoughts of resigning from this pulpit. What had I missed?

Perhaps I was looking at the world through rose-colored glasses up there. Instead of trying to get strong so I could come back and resume my role, I needed to be preparing for a quick change in my life. I became a new creature in the woods. How could I expect to come home and continue the way I had been?

I remind myself now of the many ways God speaks to me. According to

Margaret and Allison, I have to embrace God outside of the church, just as I did in the woods. I needed to look for God in all creation. The wolf, loons, snakes, eagles, bear, squirrel and deer weren't just happenstance, they were messengers!

Whew! I have so much to learn. They sure never taught me any of this in seminary.

As time went by I read and re-read my journal entries, looked over the pictures I took during my time in the woods and prayed. Seeing the photo of the loon drinking water, with a perfect mirror image reflected in the calm clear water, made me smile. I remembered how I felt sitting there watching the loon line dance, and it brought me laughter. Looking at the old dead tree stump pictures, with new flora growing in them, gave me hope. I wanted to find a way to keep myself spiritually fueled so that I would never again experience the cough...choke...sputter of a spiritual breakdown. I needed a plan that might help me to recognize false bottoms and deal with the fears that come with the deep things I cannot see.

It seemed to boil down to one primary concept for me. In order to deal with the daily challenges of life, I needed to develop healthy life priorities. In the woods, my priorities were shelter, fire and food. What were my priorities now? I needed to know what was important to me out of the woods so I could strive to keep my life in balance no matter how much things heated up.

Thinking back to the time before I went to the woods, the losses, the sadness, the draining of emotion and spirit, it is no wonder I was running on fumes. All I could think about then was, "Why is this happening to me?" As my stress level shot up, my self-esteem dropped. My life became unbalanced, and I didn't know how to recover.

What if I had developed healthy life priorities and put them into action before I ever left for Evanston, for our new church? Or even before then? What if I'd developed healthy life priorities ages ago? What if, what if. Maybe things would have been different. But I didn't, and I let the pain and sorrow grow during that time. And my trip into the woods showed me my priorities in ways that I needed to see and live. Through trial and error, I discovered my top four priorities in life. And living my truths and following the paths to those priorities has been a kind of salvation for me.

So, what are these priorities and how do they work for me?

LIFE PRIORITY #1
My first life priority is God.

> *When asked what the greatest commandment is Jesus replied,*
> "Love God with all your heart and with all your soul and with all your mind. This is the first and greatest commandment."
>
> — MATTHEW 22:37-38

It was in the woods that I began to learn that if I gave God the top priority in my life, I would have everything I needed; not everything I wanted, but the things I *needed*. Because God hadn't been first in my life, I was out of balance. And that imbalance led to everything falling apart when life heated up. My spiritual life had become like the false bottom on that back part of Bear Head Lake. I needed to get honest with myself, get past the outward shallow appearance, and go deeper like the loons were telling me. It was in the woods that I also realized my fear of deep things; things I couldn't see or understand clearly. But if God was the top priority in my life, I didn't need to fear the deep things because somehow God was IN the deep things.

As I continued living my life, I began to search out how I might maintain my newly established relationship with God, keeping God as my top priority. Clearly, being in a relationship with God must be similar to being in a relationship with anyone. And what does it take to be in a relationship with others, to keep them a priority?

First, there needed to be communication. Ultimately, prayer is nothing more than communication with God, speaking and then listening, then responding and listening more. I thought about my times of prayer in the woods and realized that they occurred more than I would have thought. I had been praying while hiking through the woods, catching a macro-zoom shot with my camera, sitting at the campfire, chopping wood, catching fish, and even while sitting out another thunderstorm. My life had become a prayer because I saw God in everything and there was little to distract me from God.

A second aspect of being in a relationship is spending quality time together. I began to realize that it's not just the amount of time we spend with God; it's also the quality of that time. For me, that time required being alone with God and embracing the silence. I needed to be intentional about quality time spent with God daily, and it definitely required a once-a-year spiritual retreat alone in the woods where I could assess my life and regroup as necessary.

I had been guilty of believing that since I was a pastor of a church, I spent most of my day centered around God. The truth is that I spent a lot of time doing work for God, but that doesn't equate to spending quality time with God.

I realized I needed to place honesty and integrity into my relationship with God. It took a spiritual crisis for me to realize that my life was a mess. I had not been honest with God, or anyone, about what was going on inside of me. I was caught up in a false sense of pride that made me believe that as a pastor I was supposed to be a spiritual cut above the rest. Once I got honest about how I was operating on spiritual fumes and found the integrity to admit it openly and ask for help, my life began to get better.

I had believed it was easier for me to keep plugging away at life without being honest about my grief and pain. After all, when I lost the sight in my eye, I was questioning whether the condition might be a punishment or a lesson from God. I didn't know how to ask God the honest questions I needed to ask. I certainly didn't know how to listen for a response. And I didn't seem to have the integrity to trust in God and not the words of others.

I heard people tell me that I shouldn't grieve for those who had died, that I was being selfish and self-centered; that I should rejoice that they were in heaven and get on with my life. I believed them and didn't trust in God to help me. It wasn't until I was deep in the woods that I got honest with God and admitted my utter pain and confusion. It's no wonder that my spiritual life had built up to the same appearance as a lake with a false bottom.

Good relationships need time for intimacy and quiet times. Barb and I had learned that as parents, we must set aside time for quiet and intimate moments together. In the same way, I needed to seek out intimate and quiet times with God on a daily basis.

Placing God as my top priority, also meant that, to preserve and grow the relationship, I needed to know as much as I could about God. Why wouldn't I want to know as much as I could about my creator, lover of my soul, and life sustainer? This would, of course, take me outside of what I had always believed about God growing up. This type of knowing was a part of going deeper, the message of the loons. It meant moving beyond my spiritual comfort zone to learn more about God in contexts other than my own.

I began to develop a personal time with God each and every day that typically involves lighting a candle and journaling. I might use prayer beads, read from devotional books, play my djembe, and set out sacred objects such as a Bible, stones, my medicine bag and/or medicine bundle. I might choose to smudge, burn sweet grass or participate in other rituals. I might choose to have this time in the house or in my prayer garden. I might sit on a chair, on the floor, or outside in the middle of a tobacco or cornmeal circle. During this time, when I speak with God, I take time to listen. I attempt to respond to what I believe I have heard, then listen some more. In addition, I take time to offer God my gratitude for everything I can think of and end with a promise to look for God in everything and everyone.

One of the greatest gifts I received in the woods was the realization that God is everywhere and in everything. In the past, I had limited my view to simply "God is in my heart". Now I can see that while God was in my heart, I was *in the heart of God*. I was inside of God and could sense the breath of God moving within the realm of nature all around me; in and out, with rhythm and balance.

Yes, this One who created me, loves me and sustains me, also dwells within and all around me. This is the One who should be the first priority in my life.

PRIORITY #2

My second life priority is my SELF.

Jesus gave us not one, but two great commandments. Let's return to Matthew 22:37-38 and add verse thirty-nine:

> "And the second is like it: 'Love your neighbor as
> yourself'".

Sometimes we confuse loving ourselves with self-indulgence, selfishness and being self-seeking. This is how I viewed self-love and self-care before going into the woods. Today I can see that if I take care of myself, I will have a lot more to give to others.

Think about the last time you rode on an airplane. Remember the safety speech given by the flight attendants? There is a part that goes something like this:

> *Should we experience a change in cabin pressure an oxygen mask will*
> *appear from the overhead bin. Place the mask over your own nose and*
> *mouth first before assisting small children or others around you.*

The first time I flew with our six-month-old, Zach, I just knew that these instructions weren't for me. I knew that if the oxygen masks appeared I would care for my son first! Then one evening at a social gathering I listened as a flight attendant talked about his job. He told a story about the plane plummeting and the oxygen masks appearing. According to him, several people ignored the instructions and tried to assist those around them first. The problem was that everyone was panicked and if you can imagine people trying to place an oxygen mask over someone else's nose and mouth you can see the problem. He told us that numerous people passed out before the pilot was able to regain control over the aircraft. This would have been prevented if people had taken care of themselves first. Then they would have been in a position to help others who might have panicked and been unable to help themselves.

I came to be in a crisis of spirit because I hadn't been taking care of myself. As a result, others were beginning to struggle, including my family and the faith community.

How am I to bind up the broken hearted and set the captives free (Isaiah 61), make disciples (Matthew 28) and feed the sheep (John 21) if I am not taking care of myself?

It became evident to me that if I didn't learn how to love and care for myself, I could never really understand how to love and care for anyone else.

Looking at the scriptures, I read Psalm 139:13-14 and realized that God created me, and God loves me. God, therefore, expects me to take care of myself. Making myself my second priority fits in with how I view God as my first priority.

"It was you, O God, who made me in my inmost self; you knit me together in my mother's womb. I praise you, for I am fearfully and wonderfully made."

I learned during my spiritual crisis and time in the woods *self* has five major parts: Physical, Mental, Emotional, Sexual, and Spiritual.

To take care of myself, to place myself as a priority, I need to practice good self-care in all these areas of self. To honor my second priority I need to, at a minimum, eat well and exercise, challenge my mind, allow my emotions to come to the surface, and deal with them in the here and now, practice the healthy sexuality that God gifted me, and openly explore spirituality. Working towards these goals gives me structure and helps me build a relationship with myself.

LIFE PRIORITY #3
My third life priority is my family.

> "If anyone does not know how to manage their own
> family, how can they take care of God's church?"
>
> — I TIMOTHY 3:5

To this day I regret not going home for my brother's funeral. Had I not been in a crisis of spirit, it would have likely occurred to me to take our son and fly to Pennsylvania, to be of support to my mother and to have my own grief process. It also would have allowed for Barb to work during the day and still have connections with the realtor.

Unfortunately, I didn't have healthy life priorities in place at that time. If I had, I would have crated Toby and brought him with us, knowing that once we got settled into our new home he would adjust and be fine. In the worst-case scenario, I could have boarded him with a vet near our new home until we got settled in. But I didn't have family as a priority, and as a result, there was a great deal of pain. These family issues were two major tactical errors I made in the move to our new city, and they were not without repercussions.

I remembered the beaver I saw swimming towards his dam, on Bear Head Lake, and thought about its commitment to family and home. I have learned that my family must be a priority in my life. When I put the church and other organizations and activities in front of them, there will be a price to pay.

Life is short! Do I want to be known for the service plaques draping my walls or for being a loving partner and mother? I have come to believe that a child raised well is the most important profession I could hold. My family must be one of my top priorities in my life.

PRIORITY #4
My fourth priority is the church

> "Keep watch over yourselves and all the flock of which
> the Holy Spirit has made you overseers. Be
> shepherds of the church of God, which he bought
> with his own blood."
>
> — ACTS 20:28

Two revelations came out of the woods with me, that I must share.

First of all, I recognized that my life priorities were in the wrong order, an unhealthy order. They needed to be reordered. Before going into the woods, I prioritized the church, my family, myself, and God. And that order led to some unfortunate life choices.

With the church as my priority, I asked my family to travel for two days to get to a city where we didn't have a home because the church needed me to get there. I found a new home for our cat because I didn't want to impose on any of the people from our new church. I didn't go home for my brother's funeral because the church would be upset if I left for Pennsylvania two days after my arrival.

I gave the church way too much power! This wasn't healthy for me or for my family, and it wasn't healthy for the church. After returning from the woods, I had first-hand experience with what happened when I moved the church out of the first-place position in my life. Those first weeks back, the meeting with the bishop and my resignation were draining experiences. But I met them with strength. I knew that God was calling me to resign within a very short time after my return. While in the woods I believed that I would either return spiritually renewed OR resign my pulpit and possibly my credentials. Instead, I returned renewed, which empowered me to resign my position with the church.

My second revelation was that I confused the church with God. Since my ministry in the church involved preaching, caring for the sick, and pastoral and theological conversations, I had internally confused my ministry, my church, with God. Putting the church first makes sense when I believed that. However, doing God's work within a structure is not the same as having a relationship with God. Somehow, over time, these concepts of God and church became intertwined, and I thought that my relationship with the church equated to my relationship with God. This can be detrimental to the life of a pastor. It certainly was to mine.

Today I recognize that the Christian church is a vessel through which people gather for worship and to carry out the work and teachings of Jesus. The church, however, is not God.

So those are my current top four priorities as I come out of the woods, renewed and recharged. If asked to list the next priorities in my life I would have to tell you that my work would be one and my friendships the other. They would likely jockey for position depending on the situation on any given day.

My work is not all-inclusive in the care for the church; it might also include studying, researching, writing, and personal retreat times that can benefit the church overall but are not particular to the church. These are things that nourish and nurture me as a pastor, then come back to nourish and nurture the congregation, through me.

Friendships are also very important in my life. I am one of those people who value and treasure my friends, and I strive to make them a priority in my life. Living priorities is an ongoing opportunity and challenge. And somedays priorities change.

Here's an example: I had a very busy workday planned, but received a call from a family member the day before, saying she would be at a nearby hospital for several hours waiting for her loved one to have some medical tests performed. I knew that I had a million things to do, and it added stress for me to think about taking time off from getting them done. However, this medical situation might be serious, and I could hear the concern and fear in her voice over the telephone. So, in this situation I decided to set aside several hours, the next day, to go to the hospital and sit with this family member, offering support. My point is, there must be some flexibility involved in these priorities from time to time.

But is it realistic to believe that I could once again get caught up in a pattern of unhealthy priorities? Is it possible that I could find myself once again going down the same road, ignoring the warning light? The truth of the matter is that, sadly enough, this will likely happen. No one is perfect.

So what do I do when I recognize that....choke...chug...sputter..... when I've waited too long, let my priorities go by the wayside, and procrastinated in remedying the situation? What do I do when I realize that I'm so afraid of the deeper issues in my life, that I've once again built up for myself a false bottom theology?

I guess the only real option for me would be to go back to the woods once again. And I know exactly where I'd point the Jeep!

There are special places in our lives that live on forever. Just entering there in memory makes them live again. We feel the heat and the cold, catch the fragrance so familiar, the aroma of certain foods, or even hear a bit of song. There are too many reasons to count, too many feelings, for us ever to lose touch with some part of us that was then--and is now".

— JOYCE SEQUICHIE HIFLER - *A CHEROKEE FEAST OF DAYS*

BACK TO THE WOODS
TEN YEARS LATER

Once again, I experienced the magic as soon as I turned off Highway 169 onto the winding road that led seven miles back through the woods to Bear Head Lake State Park. I was grateful that over the years they'd paved this seven-mile stretch. It was nice to watch for wildlife without eating dust.

My family had moved back home to Minnesota ten months prior, and the six-and-a-half-hour drive wasn't nearly as challenging as driving two to three days to get there.

There were some differences this time around. Due to a diagnosis of Fibromyalgia, I was pulling a pop-up tent trailer rather than pitching the tent. I was still staying in a non-electric site, just using the pop-up to sleep in. My back could no longer take sleeping on the ground, or the stooping to get in and out of the tent.

The other change was that I'd given up the boat and motor and become a paddler. My kayak was securely tied to the roof rack on my Jeep Wrangler. Its brilliant colors of red, orange and yellow looked like an Ely sunset. Everything else was securely packed inside the Jeep.

Spotting a deer with two fawns on the windy drive, I stopped to take a photo, but they were already meandering back into the dense underbrush, disappearing into the towering red pine and birch. Smiling, I continued the drive.

I needed this trip. It had been a whole year since my last spiritual retreat, and I was wound up tighter than the snares on a snappy drum. There had been major changes in my life over the past year. I'd accepted a pulpit in Minnesota, and moved my family, including our dog and cat (although not any of the pets we took to Oklahoma), to a new city and house.

Our twelve-year-old had been adamant that he didn't want to leave his friends and our Texas home of seven years.

"C'mon, Mama," he pleaded. "I've gone to school with these friends since kindergarten. I want to go to high school with them too!"

On top of that, shortly before we moved, we'd decided to help our eighteen-year-old dog, Sunny (sister to Allie), cross over the rainbow bridge since her health was rapidly failing and she was showing signs of suffering. She had been with us all but the first four weeks of her life, so this was a big loss to our family. Thank God for a gentle and loving veterinarian who allowed us to hold her as we said our goodbye.

Fortunately, we had an easy move and a smooth closing on the new house. It was nestled in a tree-filled lot at the base of a wooded bluff. In addition, there was a three-season porch on the back of the house where one could sit and watch the deer, squirrels, and birds from only twenty feet away. It was wonderful to be home in Minnesota! Brad and Gary, who had encouraged us to come back to Minnesota over the years, along with Barb's family, were thrilled to have us back.

Zach started junior high school three weeks later, and his teachers reported that he was only the "new kid" for about three days. A social kind of guy, he made friends quickly. Thank God!

Barb had a job lined up prior to our moving and was excited to get to work. And it was a real blessing for us to be living within an hour and thirty minutes of her family rather than a two-day drive!

I settled into the new church as a part-time pastor while working to finish my Doctorate in Ministry. In my application for the church, I had boldly stated my life priorities. I talked about these priorities again when we met for contract negotiations. I didn't want any surprises later in our ministry together. They weren't too sure about the idea of giving me time each year for a week-long spiritual retreat, but I was adamant that it was non-negotiable. Out of respect for their concern, I agreed that I would pastor with them for a whole year before taking my first spiritual retreat time. This retreat time was, in addition to paid vacation time, so I could understand their confusion.

Our family thrived in our first Minnesota winter. Zach became an avid snowboarder and took to the slopes like a Lutheran to green Jello. Barb and I were happy we'd selected a house with a wood-burning fireplace. Many Minnesota homes had switched to gas fireplaces, but we wanted to smell the wood fire. We'd forgotten how good chili tastes in the winter.

Six months later the snow appeared to be gone for the season and we were moving into temperatures in the sixties and seventies. I knew it was time to point the Jeep northward and take my spiritual retreat time. Though I didn't officially have this time in my contract yet, I just took vacation time. All I knew was that I needed to get to Ely.

This trip to Bear Head Lake marked twenty years since I'd first found this sacred space. It marked ten years since I had gone there in a spiritual crisis and two years since I'd last gone there by myself for retreat. The year before, we took a family trip to the park. It was Zach's first experience in the woods. As with most pre-teens, he didn't get it. He had a sacred moment, however, when an eagle swooped over our canoe and grabbed a fish from the water about twenty feet in front of us.

"Wow," exclaimed our young man. "That was majestic! I'll remember this moment for the rest of my life."

But now I was back here by myself. Pulling up to the beautiful new ranger station, I took a deep breath as I knew I would soon be checked in and ready to enter into the heart of the Great Spirit. The head ranger came out to greet me.

"Good to see you back! Where are you traveling from this time?" he asked with a smile.

"The great state of Minnesota!" I cried. "We've moved to southeastern Minnesota!"

"Wonderful!" he exclaimed. "We'll expect to see a lot more of you. Say now, that's a nice kayak up there on the roof."

"Well," I said slowly, "I want to honor the earth. Polluting her with all that gas didn't seem very respectful."

He nodded his approval.

"Enjoy your week. Let us know if you need anything."

With that, he was off in one direction, and I was off in the other.

Two hours later, the campsite was set up with just about everything in its place. The Memorial Day crowd was gone and there were less than ten campsites occupied, none of them anywhere near mine.

There it was: *that deafening silence*. I put down the diet cola with lime and got out of the camp chair to busy myself. Let's see. I could go get some ice and firewood, fill the water jugs, go put the leeches into the lake...

I was doing it again. It was my usual time of decompression that occurred each and every time I went to Bear Head Lake. Whether I was running on fumes or totally fueled up, the first forty-eight hours there were usually challenging as I remembered how to be alone with myself once more. I've learned over the years that a spiritual retreat is a *process*, not a destination.

I raised my hand to my neck and felt the medicine bag securely tied there as if a necklace. I pulled out my medicine bundle made of deer skin and began to unpack all its contents wrapped within a rabbit skin. Ah, there it is! The stone from last year's trip to Bear Head Lake. I held it tight in my hand and silently thanked it for the energy it had brought me over the past year. I then gave it a good throw into the woods, knowing that another would volunteer to come home with me for the coming year, before the week's end.

Finding the white sage bundle and leather pouch holding the loose tobacco, I prepared for a welcoming ceremony. The fire was sparking to life as I prepared the dried leaves of mint, cedar, yarrow and white sage. I added sweet grass to the mix along with some tobacco. Placing it on the fire to burn, I gave thanks for the campsite and all of the plants, stones and other living creatures whom I was joining. I asked for them to receive me as I settled into their space, a guest, for the coming week.

Starting with the far edge of the campsite, I walked its circumference, the lit sage bundle smoking in my hand with large plumes of grayish-white smoke. As I walked, I asked for the blessing of the Creator on the campsite. I also asked for protection throughout my stay. I knew the fierce storms that can suddenly brew up in northeast Minnesota that time of year.

When I'd smudged the whole campsite, I smudged the Jeep, the kayak, the pop-up, the food, kindling, and fishing gear. Then the rest of the smudge stick went into the fire with the other gifts.

The scent of the burning fire was intriguing. I breathed in the mix along with the fresh woodsy air. I sensed the presence of my spirit guide and thanked him for being there with me.

I'd become aware of him shortly before my mother's death a few years prior while pastoring a church in Texas. I believed him to be different from my guardian angels, a present guide sent by the Spirit to walk my earthly journey with me. His presence always reflected the Holy and pointed the way to the Creator. It was unsettling at first, like my initial experience with the medicine bag all those years ago, but once again, over time, I had embraced his presence.

Allison Snow Owl moved to Arkansas the year after we left Oklahoma, and Margaret Raven Feather moved to Florida two years after that. I missed my teachers, but their work with me was complete. They disappeared from my life the same way the feather disappeared from my medicine bag ten years ago. They taught me the basics and I learned how to trust my relationship with the Great Spirit. I knew they would be pleased I had begun my retreat with a ceremony.

Using some stones I'd brought with me from home, I built a

Medicine Wheel on the ground near the fire scar. I knew I would fill it with gifts that were presented to me during the week.

Stripping down to my shorts and an A-shirt, I began the search for kindling. The sun was shining overhead as I stacked the wood and covered it with a tarp. I sat to watch the fire die down as I picked up the neglected can of cola.

An assault by deer flies and mosquitoes led me to an anointing of my body with bug spray. Yep! I was really back.

As I watched the burning coals die, I pulled a small drum from the back of the Jeep, and quietly drummed my gratitude.

My theology had shifted over the years. Looking back, I realized that a circular path best described my theological journey over the course of my life. I grew up attending both a Hungarian Presbyterian church and the Catholic Church as a child. Although my family belonged to a church, I learned the most about God from my father while out in the fields planting corn, high up on the fender of a huge John Deere tractor.

My father would say, "Oh, look at those gorgeous clouds and that brilliant sunset. It looks as though Mother Nature painted the sky."

On one occasion he brought the tractor with the attached corn planter to a slow and grinding halt, pointing out the large slithering black snake going across our path.

"It's just an old black snake," I said with a shudder.

My father replied, "Our creator made the snakes just the same as everything else. Everything has a purpose in life, including the snakes that help the farmers by eating the field mice."

Another time he stopped the tractor to point out a pheasant nest just to the side of the field.

He said, "We won't go any closer; we don't want to disturb that mother and her nest."

My favorite memory was the time he stopped the tractor and got down to walk over to a brilliant green corn stalk coming up in the field. Smiling, he reached out, and from the midst of the leaves on that nearly six-foot stalk, he grasped a beautiful shiny black arrowhead.

He smiled as he said, "See the gifts you can find when you keep your eyes on all of God's creation?"

In retrospect, my father opened more doors to God than I ever had opened in Sunday school or Sunday worship. At least none of it ever made as much sense as my father's God-talk.

As an adolescent, I became involved in a fundamentalist Christian church where I learned that there were rules involved in being a Christian and certain prayers to pray that would get me into heaven. I was told that this was the right way to believe, and I found myself closing the doors on my father's theology.

"Dad, it doesn't matter about all this creation stuff and the animals and trees and clouds. It's not about Mother Nature. What matters is that you accept Jesus Christ as your personal savior and ask him to forgive your sins."

In that moment I suspect Jesus wept.

I stayed fundamentalist in my theology for the next twenty years, despite my issues involving my sexual orientation. I suspected that I was a lesbian at an early age but believed that I was going to hell if I ever acted on my feelings. I remember prayer sessions to heal me from homosexuality, and deliverance sessions to remove demons of homosexuality from me. I remember hearing the preachers say that no one was born a homosexual, it was either an illness or demons. When God neither healed me nor delivered me, I did not know what to believe. I also didn't know where I fit into life; I lived a lie with my Christian friends, but I didn't seem to fit into the gay culture either because I didn't know any gay Christians at that time.

Years later I came to terms with my sexual orientation and came to believe that God created me to be a lesbian and that God wants me to celebrate my sexuality. I studied the scriptures traditionally used to denounce homosexuality, and once I could study them, contextually, I found peace. However, I still held to fundamentalist beliefs about the rest of the scripture.

These beliefs began to wane when I went through the spiritual crisis that led me to the woods ten years ago. That little leather bag opened the door to a new spiritual journey for me that, over the next ten years, returned me to the creation theology of my father. I had gone full circle.

Today, I have my own personal statement of faith. It is not based on any particular creed or religious beliefs but on the evolution of my spiritual journey throughout the years. At one time in my life, I would have been fearful that any beliefs outside of fundamentalist Christianity would have damned me to hell. But today I believe that every being on this earth has their own personal spiritual journey. All roads lead home.

Further, I believe that each of us holds a tiny piece of a puzzle. Were we to put all the pieces together, I believe we would see the face of God. When we refuse to allow others' puzzle pieces to be joined with ours, we further remove ourselves from the greater picture of the Creator. This means, of course, that I must be willing to place my piece of the puzzle next to the piece provided by the black snake, should that be what the picture calls for.

To walk through the doors of my personal theology one only needs to walk through the doors of my home office. This space reflects a great deal about my personal spiritual beliefs; it is likely a curiosity to anyone who enters. One wall is devoted to non-traditional crosses through the ages including a Celtic cross, a Jerusalem cross, a cross of St. Bridgette from Ireland made from straw, and a unique Byzantine cross. On another wall hangs a peace pipe, a picture of the Spirit Christ, a hand-made choker, a rattle, a medicine bundle made from a large turtle shell, and a basket made from the pelt of a wolf. Inside the basket are medicine supplies such as sage, cedar, mint, yarrow, sweet grass and more. In the corner stands my lodge pole. On this pole hang items that reflect my individual spiritual beliefs.

Other walls in the room hold pictures of my personal spirit

animals. The most prominent images are of deer, hawks, wolves, bears, and eagles.

A table stands as a modern altar. It is not, however, a traditional Christian altar. On it, you will find a porcupine quill, a rock from the Crazy Horse Memorial in the Black Hills of South Dakota, various shells, holy water from Lourdes of France, a vial of healing oil, moss agate, a medicine bundle bound in leather, a chalice and paten made of clay, a potsherd from Israel, earth from Nazareth, a star of David, and various stones and minerals.

A small Buddha meditates on my desk. He sits serenely, holding a candle, beside the wind chimes I use for meditation.

A picture of the Last Supper hangs over the doorway. This is not a traditional picture of Jesus and the twelve sitting at a long table. Instead, it depicts Jesus, appearing to be very Jewish in appearance, at a low table where men, women and children are gathered around, and everyone is sitting on the floor.

The bookshelves in my office are lined with an eclectic assortment of reading material. While one shelf holds twelve-step studies, another holds an assortment of Bibles, the Tanakh, the Book of Mormon, and a Jewish New Testament. Other readings include women's studies, gay and lesbian studies, Native American studies, and an assortment of Christian church resource materials.

I have come to believe that God is the ultimate Creator of the universe, one God with many names, working in and through creation with an ever-present, though often invisible, evolution. I believe that God is always at work in the world through the greater picture as well as the minute details of life. I see God in the sunrise, and I see God in the smile of a child. I believe that God is Emmanual, God with us, in every aspect of life. God comes to us through the Holy Presence or Holy Spirit. This is the aspect of God we sense when we are being guided, comforted, or simply in the presence of the Holy. I believe that Jesus is a way, a truth and a life and that everyone can come to God through him. I do not, however, limit him as the only way to God. I believe that we are all sons and daughters of God and that the Divine can be found in each of us. I believe that

God has sent those who will become bridges, from our world to God. These bridges include Jesus, Mohammed, and the Buddha, among others. I believe that bridges are to be crossed, not worshipped. While I am grateful for them and for their spiritual guidance, I do not equate them with God. There have been recent times when I have questioned whether there is anything beyond the teachings of Jesus which identifies me as a Christian. And if not, how can I continue to pastor a congregation? It is a reasonable question.

This is a far cry from the fundamentalist theology of my youth. Today I celebrate the diversity of God's creation and the diversity of God's people. I no longer believe that we must say a special prayer using special words to get to heaven. Instead, life is about a relationship with the Great Mystery, and all of creation.

My evolving beliefs have moved me from the foot of the cross to the table of Jesus, where everyone is welcome. Further, I believe that each of us has a spiritual journey that we specifically choose before we come into this world. Some of us will seek and find it while others will not. I do not, however, believe that there is a beginning and end to one's spiritual life, but rather it is an eternal journey.

Today I honor my father the farmer, Mother Nature, and God the Creator, by attending to all creation. I provide water in the birdbath for the tiny fawn that wanders our back woods, abandoned after its mother was killed by a car. I gently cup the moth in my hands, that has found its way indoors, and place it back outside where it belongs. With love and care, I tend to the newly planted trees and bushes outside my window. With love and appreciation, I hold the people of our congregation, placed in my pastoral care, in my heart and in my prayers. I strive to model God's all-inclusive love and to offer sermons and worship opportunities in which to observe and join in the full celebration of God's diversity in creation. Further, I remind them of their joy when finding a church with an open door and of our responsibility to keep that door open just as wide for everyone else. With the words of my father, I implore them to: "See the gifts you can find when you keep your eyes on *all* of God's creation?"

. . .

It was a marvelous week in the woods filled with hiking, kayaking, fishing, journaling, and lots of photo opportunities. I heard there were two moose cows seen early in the morning by Cub Lake, but try as I might, I never spotted them. One morning as I drove into town for my annual breakfast at the Chocolate Moose, I spotted a Timber Wolf running across the road in front of me. I was so excited I could hardly breathe.

On another day I drove over to another lake located in the park. Eagles Nest 3 is a beautiful lake. I'd seen it before, but I'd never been on it. As I drove down the road I could hear the straps, holding the kayak in place, slapping on the roof. Finding it irritating, I pulled over on the narrow road with a large lake right beside me. I left the Jeep running and walked around to the passenger side to tighten the straps. Just as I had the second one secured tightly, I glanced around the Jeep to see a HUGE bear lumbering out of the woods. He had to have weighed at least six-hundred pounds if he weighed an ounce. I quietly tried to open the passenger side door and slip into the Jeep. It was locked. On one side of me, just a couple of feet away, was the lake. My choice was to jump in the lake or try to move quickly and quietly around to the driver's side of the Jeep. Peering through the windows I could see this giant looking curiously at the Wrangler. I moved into his view and heard him snort.

"Hey there!" I called out in a friendly voice. "How are you? I'm just going to pop into my Jeep here and move right along, OK?"

Baffling him with my bullshit seemed to be effective. He stood there on all four watching me as I slipped into the driver's side. With a new sense of bravado, I grabbed my camera and snapped off three shots before he lumbered off into the woods.

Prior to my leaving Evanston, my precious teachers presented me with a gift that would keep on giving. The book *Animal Speak* by Ted Andrews, added to the sacred experiences because it gave meaning to the various animals, birds, and reptiles. I'd already looked up loon, eagle, squirrel, fox, turtle, deer, and wolf, that week. I knew better than to ignore the significance of these animals that came into my life. I couldn't wait to get back to my campsite and look up information about the bear!

The medicine wheel was also filling up with various objects. My favorite was a piece of driftwood in the shape of a cross. It actually looked as though a cloth draped it. There were also some shells, a beautiful flower I'd found uprooted, and some stones. I'd added tobacco, sage and sweet grass to it as well.

Journal Entry:

It was a rainy morning. The skies let loose, and it just poured after breakfast. I sat inside the pop-up, grateful for dry shelter. At least it didn't storm. It cleared out by noon, and I decided to hike around Norberg Lake.

I returned to the campsite by late afternoon and decided on a nap before starting the fire for supper. The skies were blue all afternoon but it's clouding up again.

Sadly, I find myself moving toward a schedule again. I'd like to be on the road by 9:00 tomorrow morning so I'll miss rush hour in the Twin Cities. I'd also like to be home in time to go to Zach's soccer game. I will organize and pack what I can this evening.

I'll watch for moose as I leave the park tomorrow. I'll leave my camera out just in case.

I pulled out of the park at 8:30 the next morning. The medicine wheel was dismantled, and the site left even cleaner than I'd found it. A new stone had made its way into the medicine bag and would journey with me over the coming year. I'd blessed the lake, the leeches, the campsite and all the stones and vegetation that had surrounded me while I was there. What a glorious week! My skin was tan, my body stronger, and my spirit refreshed. I didn't see any moose, but there's always next year! There's always a good reason to come back to Bear Head Lake State Park!

And as I turned onto 169 South, I realized that I was out of the woods once again.

At least for now.

AFTERWORD

Go to hangarıpublishing.com to learn more about the Author and stay up to date with their newest releases.

ACKNOWLEDGMENTS

I would like to thank Kathryn Johnson, the amazing writer, editor and owner of Write by Me, who shared her editing expertise in an earlier version of this book. In addition, I would like to thank Carol Berteotti for lending her extraordinary editing expertise to this later version.

I would like to acknowledge Bear Head Lake State Park for seeing me through many joys and challenges over the last forty years. I especially thank the park rangers and staff, particularly Jody Popesh, who assisted with editing and obtaining permission for me to use the state park's name.

I would also like to thank Jeep© for creating my turquoise '97 Wrangler Sport that offered me ten years of driving fun and adventure both in the woods and out of the woods.

www.ingramcontent.com/pod-product-compliance
Lightning Source LLC
Chambersburg PA
CBHW071152120626
46546CB00006B/2227